Mary Sthart

£1.49

1/7

G000090840

Henry

Elizabeth Yandell

('The Blister')

ILLUSTRATED BY

Faith Jaques

THE BODLEY HEAD
LONDON SYDNEY
TORONTO

God gave us memory
in Springtime
that we might have roses
in December

Kent 1894   Jersey 1973

CHAPTER ONE

I was one year old when I fell for Henry. Thereafter I was his
devoted slave. It was on record and a standing joke, that when
I became aware of him as a person, distinct from all others who
prodded my middle in passing, I squirmed right round in my
bassinet and pitched out over the hood. Seeing me squalling
at his feet, he picked me up and dumping me back amongst the
covers legged it for the potting-shed as fast as the wheels would
turn. Once in safety he made certain there was no damage, sat
me down on a heap of sifted soil, gave me a couple of thumb-
pots and a trowel to play with and got on with his job at the
bench. I had begun gardening.

To Authority, Henry was the Sergeant, with punctilio.

In the Bothy he was known, affectionately, as the Old Cock; the lads said he was always clucking and crowing. It was funny, it never entered my head to wonder about his age. He never seemed any older, although he was seventy-five when he died. He never owned to more than twenty-one. To Cookie, he was 'that dratted head gardener'. Each morning at nine the kitchen was a battleground, bayonets fixed. Henry opined that she was 'a Brass Bound old besom'. She pinched his thunder, prowling the gardens every night after dinner was over and, mortal sin, she had even been seen helping herself. This was all wrong. Tradition, and a head gardener's dignity, demanded that a housekeeper, no matter how august, asked, fairly humbly, what was ready for the house. Cookie didn't. She knew, and told him so, without preamble: it didn't make for sweet harmony. One thing foxed her though. The keys of the greenhouses were always in Henry's pocket. Peep she might, but couldn't pry. The situation amused Authority. He backed Henry. Not openly, for she was a pearl of price, and she knew it. An expert cook and housekeeper; and, as today, those were not thick on the ground. He knew who grilled the steak, and the daily battles went on.

To me, Henry was mine, my alley marble, Fides, ever present help in troubles or puzzles. My own dear Liz was Henry's wife, with a very special place in my heart. She had fastened all my first safety-pins; taught me my prayers; starched my frills; dosed me at need with castor oil; saw to it that I toed the ladies' line; and when necessary spanked me. She had a hard hand, and a sense of justice. Also, oh! humble pie, she plastered my finger-nails with bitter aloes, but bad as I was she loved me. She said so, often. Many years later she told me I had been the trial of her life, a regular demon. Recalling a very early tussle in a fashionable London shop over the purchase of my first parasol for a smart wedding, I knew she spoke the truth.

That incident stayed with me down the years. She had slapped me—publicly! At four-and-a-half years old, even a

(8)

prospective bridesmaid has no aesthetic sense. I was to have a parasol. For me! Oh my! An armful was placed upon the counter. I seized a frightfully exciting yellow affair, with a frill round the top and a crazy pattern of fairytale characters, all the colours of a rainbow. I wanted it! I held on to it! Mine! Mine! Said Liz, 'That's not a lady's parasol.' No! No! No! She pulled. I pulled. I opened my mouth and made a roaring shindy. Shocking behaviour! Customers backed away. We were left on a carpeted desert. Then it was that Liz, red-faced and disgraced, slapped me, hard! I was so outraged that I stopped screeching. She said, 'If you have that yellow thing, you'll have "Pompey" on your back in no time!' What a threat! That was enough for me. Pompey! On my back . . . Pompey! All kids were scared of Pompey. I left Marshall and Snelgrove's with a plain strawberry silk parasol, discreet and elegant. It had a cherrywood handle carved with a cat's head. I came to love it dearly. When Henry saw it he thoroughly approved. I did, too.

Poor, darling Liz, I must have been a little beast. No wonder Henry christened me 'The Blister'. The great friendship between us amused our guests and outsiders. He was my idol. If Henry said so, then so far as I was concerned, the last word had been said. It *was* so. He could do no wrong, nor be wrong. It was, thank heaven, to be years before I learned that he had one foot of clay. Who hasn't? Sufficient in those early years was the knowledge that my world held Henry and the endless delight of gardening beside him, crawling on all fours behind the mowing-machine long before I could stand upright.

When I'd grown a bit and had full use of my legs, Henry exploited my devotion. Authority had a thing about daisies in turf. It's pretty common today. Called a complex. Seventy odd years ago we didn't go in for complexes. You just had the fidgets. The sight of a few open eyes on the lawn was certain to release an attack of daisy fidgets on Henry's head, especially if visitors were expected. Henry couldn't win. Quite useless to explain that there was no keeping upsides with the b—y things in the country where seeds blew from the meadows, and that the boys spent most of the winter months on hands and knees spudding them out. The contest always ended with a nice display of orderly-room acidity.

After one such skirmish Henry had an idea. He presented me with an old enamelled washbowl, capacity about half a gallon, and promised me a sixpence, his whole week's 'bacca' money, if I'd go over the front grass every morning before the bedroom blinds were raised, and pick off every open daisy I could see. I liked the idea. I was just learning how to handle a money-box, thrift and whatnot. I was daft. I had a good look at the option. There didn't seem to be all that many daisies: besides, I was always up and out soon after daylight all summer long.

In a world full of early morning enchantments that was my busiest time. A brand new day. I had to let my bantams out to scratch; watch the guinea-fowls, line ahead, stringing along to the coverts, the last fowl yelling, 'Come back! Come back! Come back!' to those ahead. In early March I watched the Kentish plovers cutting capers all over the sky. 'Pee-wit. Pee-wit.' Sometimes I heard the curlews winging across making their exquisite, rippling, sweet calling. Sometimes, with real luck, I would see two or three daft old buck hares performing their dotty antics on Farmer Harvey's fallows.

Away across the front lawn there was the lake. It wasn't large as lakes go. Henry said it had once been a stew, where some religious house had bred carp for Friday fish dinners. It was lovely clear water, fed by a spring at one end, and the overflow trickled away as a brook through the meadow, to the roadside ditch beyond our boundary. According to the time of year the lake either teemed with frogs, who kept us awake at night until they'd finished courting, or pullulated with tad-poles, when the gander from Harvey's Farm brought his harem

over a mile to feast. Eels bred there too, coming and going on
their secret journeys to the sea.

A couple of herons were our constant guests, up to their
knobbly knees in the water, snapping elvers, just as herons
must have stood centuries before, waiting to gobble up some old
abbot's carp. Sometimes they left the water to stalk the lawn, all
stiff-legged and moody, withdrawn-looking. 'Indigestion! Too
many elvers!' said Henry. Then I would run across the grass
and make them fly, long necks and heads thrust out in front,
long legs hanging behind like tapes out of badly-packed baggage. They looked so funny. What matter if my legs and petticoats got wet with dew? It was worth a scolding.

To me, picking daisies was just another ploy. I stuck to the
job for a fortnight, and in spite of mowing twice a week, the
darn things gained on me. It was wonderful growing weather.
I was no nearer that sixpence. It had to go down on the drum;
the situation must be clarified. I found Henry sitting in the big
greenhouse; he was whittling labels. He listened gravely whilst
I opened negotiations.

At six years old one is still wet behind the ears. He spun me
a long yarn about the cost of Irish twist 'bacca' at threepence an
ounce. The question of the cash was evidently an error. Finance
should not be raised between friends. I had put myself out-of-
face. There was stone cold logic in the fact, that, as he was at
pains to point out, I'd never filled the bowl. I couldn't remember whether or not the bargain had included anything about
filling the bowl. I hadn't a leg to stand on. We compromised
on an early peach off the back wall and a bit of black liquorice
out of Henry's cough box. Henceforth I laboured for love and
liquorice. Somehow the tale got round to Authority; he was
much amused. He came and found us in the potting-shed,
laughed a lot with Henry, pulled my curls and said I had to learn
that the world was a very wicked place for the innocent, and
told Henry that the front grass must be mown three times a
week in future. Henry saluted. Years later I saw that he'd evened

matters up very neatly, that he too was a man of ideas. The front lawn was very large. A whole universe it seemed to me in those faraway days. Where Henry really let himself go was on bedding schemes.

Opposite the front door there was an old sundial; around it a bed full of flowers that opened and closed as the sun crossed the sky. Both plants and dial kept exact time on sunny days. It was of endless interest to me. There were other beds, full in springtime with fat blue hyacinths or flaming scarlet, yellow-edged tulips, called Keizerskroons. In summertime, a glory of Paul Crampel geraniums, yellow calceolarias, royal blue lobelias and golden yellow pyrethrums, rose-beds edged with pansies. The Abel Chatenay roses, delicately pink, were edged with Maggie Mott violas; exquisite, mauve, scented flowers, beautiful for table decoration, so easily propagated either by division or by cuttings in autumn. They seem to have entirely disappeared from cultivation. All these beds were tricky to mow between, a job Henry never trusted anyone to do but himself. I stood on the sidelines, watching admiringly as he swung the mower within a whisker of every curve, whilst the daises flew back into the grassbox. I was out of a job.

A couple of weeks later Henry suggested I might get some fun out of pulling the machine whilst he pushed. I could pretend I was a horse. He'd do all the twiddly bits and I might be better off on the straight. I would help him. I was all for being helpful. He made a broad leather belt, to fit my middle and to take a cord we tied to either side of the mower. I bent to the job, pawing and snorting like the plough horses did. Henry gee-upped and whoa-ed, and off we went. We had a strict routine: ten rows up and down, long, straight panels of green and silver, beautiful: a job well done. Five minutes' stand-easy whilst Henry stoked his cutty for two draws and a spit, before we were off again. I was happy and long sunny hours went by. I didn't really do any pulling. I only thought I did.

When the lawn was finished and a lad set to tidy the edges,

we took the machine to the cleaning-shed and saw that it was in order for the next user. My job was to hand the cleaning rags and brushes and squirt oil into all the right places, tidy away the rags, and rinse out the brushes, hanging them to dry. Everything we touched had to be left clean.

All done, we went to the stoke-holes to see that the boilers were doing their job, and on, into the hot-houses. I loved the moist, warm, growing scents in the big spans, a sort of urgent, hurry-up-and-bloom smell, sweet with the perfumes of rose geraniums, Chinese primulas, and cyclamen, musk and stephan-otis. All this beauty was in response to cow-dung plaster. Don't shudder in distaste, it wasn't as bad as it sounds. It was a form of foliar feeding, primitive maybe, but no less successful than that extensively advertised today.

It meant going to the long meadow with Henry. He took the wheelbarrow and a fork. I was only an onlooker, full of curiosity. It is amazing the insect life that can be found under half-dried cow-pats; nothing in this world is wasted. No won-der crows and starlings spend so much time turning them over. With a barrow-load of half-dried cow-pats we'd return to the garden, dump the lot in a deep tank and return for more until we had a good tankful. Water was added to soak the mass and break it down, with enough soil to make a nice plastic mess, after working with a long pole.

This plaster was laid on all the hot-water pipes, as a sort of lagging, half an inch thick, resulting in the lovely moisty fug which made things grow so wonderfully. When the nature had sweated out of the muck, it was scraped off and a fresh lot applied. Science? My foot! There's nothing new under the sun.

CHAPTER TWO

Henry kept a bottle hanging on the back of the potting-shed door, in the pocket of an old coat. I never saw him touch that bottle. Years later I was to learn that it was his private curse, a story not unusual in those days when the black sheep of a family was a pariah, the Regular Army his only anonymity. Henry, of sound yeoman stock and grammar school education, with sound prospects ahead, had gone to market on his fifteenth birthday, been encouraged to celebrate too heartily, and was carried home wildly drunk. He had struck his father, taken a horse-whipping and been slung into the hayloft by two man-servants and left to cool off.

First thing next morning, before anyone was astir, he had

walked to the county recruiting station and 'taken the shilling', gone to India with the regiment, met Authority (and married my Liz), returned to England with him and stayed on. He never went back to his own people.

Henry was not a boozer in the ordinary sense of being an everyday drunk. He was a pathological case, with a tainted inheritance. His everyday bottle was a tea-bottle; not just a barmaid's joke, it was tea. On tea he'd go along for months, until some mischance awoke his sleeping devil. Then he'd drink hard, walking miles for it, for a fortnight. Just as suddenly he'd sober up and the bout was over until the next time. He was a sick man, to be pitied not censured. Our Vicar's wife was completely unable to grasp this truth. A bigoted teetotaller, she ran the village Band of Hope, and battled relentlessly to get Henry to sign the pledge, to his great annoyance. She was never without a pocketful of little pictorial text cards, little moral jerkers, which she handed out to all and sundry. She left one in the potting-shed. Two highly-coloured little birds with the admonition, STRONG DRINK IS A MOCKER. Henry reckoned they must be mocking-birds and used the card to stop a hole in a seed tray. She was a very good vicar's wife, ran the parish and kept a mighty sharp eye on souls—especially on the youngsters.

Woe betide the maiden seen in dalliance behind a hedge with a ploughboy; she could look forward to a red-cheeked half hour at Sunday school. Woe betide the miserable schoolboy caught backing out of an orchard with his pockets full of scrumped apples. And damnation was the promised lot of any little servant girl turning up to evensong with a dusting of powder on her nose or a little bit of vain frippery. She didn't disdain a bit herself on occasions. That puzzled me. Perhaps the Lord looked kindly on vicars' wives and made exceptions? I asked Henry. He wasn't any help, really.

Cookie was also a member of the Temperance Society, very, very down on drink. She had a strong drink text tacked up on the kitchen mantelshelf. She didn't drink, but I'd noticed that when we had guests and she was cooking in a big way with wine or brandy, she always tasted what she was making; sometimes two, or even three times, before she was satisfied with the flavour. I pondered quite a lot on this, coming to the conclusion that perhaps there was someone, like the Pope, who could give special dispensations to cooks. There must be, or it just didn't make sense. I put it to my Godfather, he listened and said it seemed a sound notion.

The bigger I got the more trotting around I did. I was the 'go-for' and pleased as Punch I went, flattered and glad to be useful to my partner. He was a wily old bird. He would get up off his knees, drop his trowel, groan and sit heavily in the wheelbarrow, and rubbing his knees hard, groan, 'Oh! Oh! Poor Henry has got a bone in his leg.' Then he'd wheedle. 'You wouldn't like Henry to die thirsty because he'd forgotten to bring our tea-bottle now, would you? Your legs are younger than his. It's on the potting-bench. Nip and get it.' Henry! Die! The bare possibility of such a thing sent me running like a hare for that life-saving bottle. I had a sick horror of death and I knew it, something I never confessed to either Henry or Liz. It haunted my dreams.

Along the coppice side, where I sometimes went walking with Authority or with Liz, there was a wire fence, the keeper's larder, hung with dead varmints; where Havinden the keeper tied all the vagabonds, kestrels, weasels, stoats, rats and magpies, hedgehogs and moles, all in various stages of terrible dissolution, attended by scores of blue-bottle flies. Visions of Henry flapping there lent me speed. That was what the word dead meant to me. I had not yet become aware of coffins and graves, although, when Jenny the donkey died, we buried her in the vine border. That seemed different. The relief of finding Henry still sitting in the barrow was only equalled by the fascination of watching him drink, from the bottle. He drank gratefully, as a hen does, head well up, his Adam's apple bobbing up and down as he swallowed. I longed to see it either hit his chin or hook on to his shirt-stud. There was always the alluring chance that with an extra big swallow it might. Oh, the dotty hopes of childhood! Sometimes he would ask me to go to the shed for a forgotten tool, with the reminder to 'replace everything properly, mind!' There was really no need for that. The shed was as tidy as a barrack square, it was Henry's pride. I could lay hands instantly on anything he needed. To this day I judge a man by the state of his tool-shed.

One afternoon Authority caught me hauling the short scythe across to the lakeside. He exploded into wrath. Henry and I bowed before the storm until Authority had rumbled off back to the house. Henry remarked that we'd better be more careful for a bit, no good asking for trouble. But another day was to come when we both forgot. 'Oh! Come on, my Blister. Just nip along and fetch me the little badging hook,' said Henry: and off I went. Carefully and responsibly I started back through the kitchen garden. I could see the the blade was razor sharp. I was at peace with the world. It was a marvellous afternoon, full of mellow sunshine and the scent of ripe quinces. One of those blue-skied, magical afternoons when you can either soar with the swallows or fall face down into trouble. I came abreast of a fine row of cauliflowers, and stopped to admire them. Suddenly, heaven only knows what possessed me. Out of nowhere came the stunning conviction. They weren't cauliflowers at all! They were heads of close white curls! They were Saracens! Enemies! To be smitten, hip and thigh. The devil was in it. I was a crusader. A knight of the Holy Cross. The hook was my Toledo blade. Wahoo and St George! Oh, the sheer inconsequence of it. I raised the hook above my head, left the path for the well-hoed garden, seized the nearest cauliflower by a handful of leaves and let drive, with all the weight of my tubby seven years behind it. The hook came up through the fistful of greenery and caught my fingers. Momentum took me

round in a circle and I fell on the earth. I sat up. I was bleeding
. . . Dying . . . Nay dead! I was no hero of legend. I needed
help. I was scared. All the spit and blow left me. There before
me, plain to see, was a row of cauliflowers. I opened my mouth
to yell and remembered that I had been forbidden to touch
dangerous tools. *Esprit de corps.* The less attention I called to my
plight the better for me, and Henry. He'd know what to do. I
saved my tears until I could see his 'ard 'at above the asparagus
grass. He stared at me: not believing what he saw. He said,
'Strewth! *You ruddy Blister!* You've done it this time.' He added
a few words on strict obedience to orders. Sat me in the wheelbarrow and trundled me along to the shed. Some instinct told
me that if I was scared so was he.

Inside the shed he tied a couple of turns of twine round my
wrist and said, 'Don't move till I get back,' and vanished,
locking me in. In no time he was back again with a bowl of
clean water and a couple of strips of material, striped like his
shirt. He carefully washed and assessed the damage. More
blood than actual disaster. A couple of big spider-webs from
under the bench stopped the bleeding and with the strips of
material making all snug, the worst was over. He helped me off
with my blood-stained cotton dress, soused it in the tub we used
for washing flower-pots, wrapped me in a clean sack, sat me
on an upturned bushel basket and saying all was over, bar the
shouting, went off up to the house. He was gone quite a while.
I sat there, prey to all sorts of worries. What would Liz say?
What on earth had made me behave in such a silly fashion?
What was most important, what would Authority say? Would
he stop my working with Henry? I knew a moment of insub-
ordination. If he did, I'd run away from home. I'd go to the
gipsies. My fingers hurt. I started to snivel. I was sorry for
myself. It was beyond me.

Henry went straight to Authority and made a clean breast
of the incident. I never knew how much shouting he got; for
me there was none, not even from Liz. Fright was considered

punishment enough. Henry returned, very red in the face, with a can of hot sweet tea and a couple of freshly-baked currant buns. In the pocket of his apron he had a warm dress for me; he pulled it over my head and fastened the back buttons, poured us each a mug of tea and we sat down to a bun apiece, and munched quietly. I was grateful for that hot drink. Watching Henry spitting out the burnt currants off the top of his bun, there came to me a moment of rare illumination. I knew, with that acute clarity of vision which is the especial benison of child-hood, that Henry was one of Heaven's most truly blest people in this world whom you can trust to eternity and beyond. They are few, and they are all children at heart. Grace is around them like a cloud of glory. That moment was mine, bubble-enshrined, in time eternal. Dear, good Henry.

CHAPTER THREE

Authority and Henry were both big men, yet neither carried any spare weight. They measured up in honesty, personality and humanity. Authority stood six foot two in his socks; Henry, five foot eight. Both were born on the same communicating wavelength, and duty was a way of life. In uniform, with all their medals up, they were quite a sight. Authority always said that, but for his unfortunate inheritance, Henry would have risen high in his profession, an inspired leader of men. As it was, he was loved and trusted by all. In fact he was, on the estate, obeyed without question.

The lads he schooled in our gardens left us for their first jobs in the wider world all the better for having known Henry's influence. He was an inspiring teacher. Guide, philosopher and friend, he helped them straighten out personal problems, as well as those of their chosen profession. A friend for life.

Some, not many, got across him. A liar he could not bear. I once overheard him telling off a lad who had lied to him, his words clipped like hail on corrugated iron. 'Fleas and lies, my lad, are the fastest breeders in the world. There's never a single flea, or a lonely lie, and don't you forget it. You see to it that you never try to lie to me again or I'll kick your unmentionable arse all round the kitchen garden. Now get out. There's four boxes of lobelias waiting to be pricked out. The soil is ready. Singly, mind. Four thousand plants, and don't forget the labels. Now go to it.' When Henry said singly, he meant just that. The lad slunk away to an endless job. A task of absolute monotony. Discipline was the end product; lobelias, and reflection. Normally, two lads would have been set to the business of pricking out, so that they could chat. Not this time.

Today there is no discipline, and life is out of kelter thereby. To Henry, all boys were army rookies, they had to be properly shaped. Pruned, was his word. If he bore down on them when they asked for it, he was also free with praise when due; and they had every encouragement from him. If they wanted to become good head gardeners they had first to serve; if you can't obey, was his maxim, you'll never command.

Our front drive was three hundred yards from gate to forecourt; every yard of gravel was raked each morning before breakfast. Every lad took a turn, a week at a time; that, together with clipping verges, mowing, hedge clipping, planting and pricking out, seed sowing, scrubbing hundreds of dirty flowerpots. No pot was used twice without scrubbing in carbolic water. Right through the grind he led them to the ultimate pinnacle, the staging of perfect show exhibits. A thorough training; they took the lot. Alongside my beloved Henry, so did I, albeit on a far gentler scale. I scrubbed all the thumbpots.

We had a varied succession of lads, rough and smooth, and some turned out some pretty good gardeners. One lad will always live in my memory because we found him, a waif, nearly dead. Hunting with Henry for a stray cat and her kits in the loft above the stables, we found him in the hay, wet to the skin, and deeply unconscious. Henry raised him. 'Only a handful of skin and grief,' he said, as we got him down the steps to the stable and laid him on the bench. He sent me to Cookie for hot soup and water-bottles and to find Jack Dence, the under gardener. Jack was in the kitchen yard as I went through. I told him and he came in to carry the soup. Hot soup on the instant was no problem in our kitchen, where the stock-pot boiled on the range all day and every day.

When we returned to the stable Henry had rigged up a bed, stripped the sodden clothing from our discovery and rolled him into a horse blanket. We packed the hot bottles round him and piled more blankets on top. With a feeding cup Jack Dence and Cookie tried to bring back some life into the poor creature. He recovered enough to be able to swallow a few drops of chicken broth laced with brandy. When he was able to speak, he was able to tell us that he was Tom, aged fourteen, a bit of human flotsam from London's East End, determined to escape from personal miseries. Escape? To where? Oh, just anywhere. When he was a little nipper he'd been hopping in Kent with his mum. His mum? No, he'd no longer got a mum. She'd died when he was eight. Cookie was in tears. Jack Dence was coughing. It was a sordid story Henry got from him before he fetched Authority to the scene.

Compassionately Authority questioned the waif, before tell-ing Henry, 'Get him vetted. He can stay here until the doctor's been. If he's a clean bill of health, Jack's mother can take him in at the Back Lodge; she's got a little bedroom. We'll kit him out with clothing and take him on in the Bothy.' He patted Tom's head. 'There's good stuff there. Look after him, Sergeant.' Henry saluted.

'Cor!' whispered our find. 'Aint 'e a toff?'

Cookie got another cupful of soup into him and we left him to sleep. We never found those kittens.

Jack's mother, Old Mrs Dence, had borne nine children. Only one had survived, our Jack. She was a bright, sharp-eyed little woman, reminiscent of a cuddly hen robin. She bustled around and had a motherly chest. She took to our Tom as to another son, and cherished him.

He developed as a dark-eyed, pale-faced creature, gentle as a dormouse, lean, skinny and gangling. He grew but didn't seem to thrive. Mrs Dence said he was a dear good lad but he only lengthened; she couldn't widen him no how, that she couldn't.

Authority christened him 'the stick insect', just what he resembled as he squatted to trim verges round the lawns. He had a shy love for Cookie and Liz and would leave little bouquets of wild flowers on the kitchen table. Liz knitted socks for him and Cookie always baked a few extra buns for Tom. For Henry he had a devotion that was almost idolatry, copying him in everything and making desperate efforts to grow a moustache. What made them grow? He consulted Cookie privately on the question.

'A lot of hope and quite a few years,' she said. Cold comfort, little encouragement, but the truth.

Tom had been with us for a couple of years when Jack noticed he was limping badly, and so did Henry. Was he in pain? Henry questioned him. Yes, he was. Bad pain, and confessed to a boil on his buttocks. No, he hadn't told Mrs Dence. Couldn't tell a woman, wouldn't be decent, like. Nothing against Henry having a squint. Henry took him into the Bothy and bade him let down his britches. After inspecting the site he opined it was a beauty, big as an egg, just right.

Telling Tom to haul up and brace and return in half an hour, Henry came to find me. I was to go to the kitchen, ask Cookie for a clean, two-pound pickle jar, a cake of soap—

yellow, primrose, household soap—a cupful of dark-brown Barbados sugar and a bundle of old, clean, linen rags, and bring them back to the Bothy, and on the way tell Jack that Henry wanted him. I knew what was afoot. On my way across the front lawn I ran into Authority; naturally he wanted to know where I was going in such a tearing hurry. Naturally, I told him what was going on. When I returned with the needful he was there before me, consumed with curiosity.

Jack had a smart fire going in the stove, with a kettle just coming along to the boil. Authority perched himself on the table, turning his long legs well out of the way, watching Henry scraping thin slivers off the cake of soap with his pocket-knife, moistening them on a plate with a few drops of hot water and a sprinkling of Barbados sugar, working the whole into a nice paste.

The poor 'stick insect' limped in to watch Henry spreading this on a square of old, soft sheeting. He was ordered to take off his britches, let down his underpants, back to the stove and bend over a chair. The kettle was boiling heartily. Jack took the pickle jar in his hands and held the mouth over the spout, gathering the steam. I was shooed outside and the door slammed. I didn't mind; I'd seen it all before, on less private parts.

With the jar full of boiling steam, Henry held Tom down over the chair, whilst Jack clapped the mouth fair and square over the exact spot. The boil burst, as cleanly as though enucleated with a scalpel, into the steaming vacuum. Tom yelled. The Bothy door banged open, flat back. The victim, grabbing his underpants with both hands, made a screeching round of the vegetable garden without stopping. Authority, normally the kindest and most compassionate of men, was clinging to the doorpost, helpless with laughter. Henry stood beside the table holding the soap and sugar plaster as one who controls destiny, awaiting Tom's return. Then he clapped it into place, ordered him home to bed, and said he must lie on it for twenty-four hours. Swearing that he was better already, Tom went off, and in a few days had forgotten his ordeal by hot jar. It was barrack-room surgery, gipsy medicine, clean, aseptic, and amazingly effective. Jack said it was enough to put a chap off pickles for life.

Next morning Mrs Dence was astir early. She caught the carrier's cart into Cranbrook, and returned with half a gallon of barm from the brewery; she'd see he didn't get any more boils. Two tablespoons a day; brewer's barm was specific for boils, ranking even higher than brimstone and treacle as a blood purifier. Brimstone and treacle! One large tablespoonful taken fasting, every morning for a week in springtime, cleaned suety pudding complexions, spotty chins, impetigo and itch. Every country child knew this. Knock it off for a week, then do another week on the treatment. Cream and roses! Brimstone and treacle was luscious stuff when you first got your spoonful in your mouth, but it was unwieldy. It clung to your tongue and clogged your teeth. Awful, you could neither spit nor swallow. You just had to suck it down. Artful and knowledge-able kids licked away the treacle and, left with a mouthful of dry, gritty flowers of sulphur, remembered urgent business behind the woodpile and jettisoned the lot. Artful and know-ledgeable mothers lined 'em up in the kitchen and watched them swallow the lot. They weren't all winners, at least, not all the time.

Cookie had a dark reason for pimples, boils, and blains and all skin troubles. They were all, she declared, the result of inborn original sins, plain wickedness. That's how it all came out, just as the Bible said, and if naughty children told lies they got pimples on their tongues, you just see! I resolved there and then to try it out next day. I suppose there is a law of coincidence. I tried. It worked. I got a sore tongue. Thereafter, for years, I never felt quite sure about Cookie. Had she a private 'Pompey'?

After the boil incident, Tom waxed and filled out present-ably. Cookie roped him into her Bible class, and said it had done him a lot of good. Old Mrs Dence was certain it was due to the brewer's barm. Pull devil, pull brewer. I discussed this with Henry. He backed brewer's barm against the Bible class any day. 'Though, mind you,' he warned me, 'a bit of both can't do any harm.' We left it like that.

Authority never frowned upon my self-imposed apprentice-ship with Henry. What I did with myself after my book lessons were done for the day was up to me, so long as I didn't make a nuisance of myself, or get into anyone's way. Mischief? Well, mischief and I were twins. Authority hadn't really much use for a girl. A boy would have been different. Might have been raised for the regiment, instructed in the mysteries of military strategy and the ordinance manual. A girl? Out of sight, out of mind. With Henry I was safely occupied. He would sometimes potter along to the shed to see what I was up to, have a few words with Henry on politics and what have you, kiss me and bid me be good. I'd give him a hug and he'd potter off again. I loved him dearly, but he wasn't half the fun that Henry was.

Henry was such wonderful company, I learned many things from him besides garden lore. There were periods when Authority was away on spells of duty, and life not so full of estate jobs. In free time we made expeditions. Henry and Liz took me to all the historical places in the county, Sissinghurst, Rochester, Richborough, The Cinque Ports, Dover Castle, Canterbury Cathedral, and Reculver Towers where Saint Augustine landed in Kent bringing Christianity to England. Henry knew all the stories of these places, of the great ones who had built them, lived and died in them. He made it all come alive again for me.

At Reculver, below the old graveyard, west of the ruins where the channel tides were steadily eating the land, I found a piece of terracotta pottery on the stony beach. Proudly I carried it home. The Vicar said it was part of an old Roman kitchen jar, probably a Roman soldier's wine jar, hundreds of years old. Mysterious Reculver; terrible battles had been fought there. Britons, Danes, Saxons and Romans, had all been buried in the graveyard long before Augustinian monks made a holy place of it.

On the beach, before the turn of the century, after heavy winter storms, age-old arm and leg bones could be picked up, and fine relics were said to be in the hands of antiquarians, dug out on moonlight nights, and sold. A strange, restless place. For me, a little child listening to all this, Reculver ruins were part of a past to which I undoubtedly belonged, just as I was part of what was yet to be. That was a tremendous thing to hand on to a child. It gave me a strange sense of kinship. I was there, on the spot where all these things had happened. It was like seeing a picture in a frame.

In Canterbury Cathedral I stood where Thomas à Becket was slain for sticking to his principles, where he died at bad men's hands because he upheld what he saw was right. I stood beside the tomb of the noblest Prince in Christendom, the proud effigy, his armour and tattered standard. I knew awe at his exploits, humbled by his bravery. But I was sure that Henry and Authority were soldiers just as brave. Of course they didn't wear armour or wave tattered banners, but they'd smelled powder. I swelled with pride inside myself. Some day I'd be brave, just like the Black Prince. But I wasn't. When, minutes later, we were out in the cloisters, in that dark entry where they buried Nelly Cook 'with a mouldy piece of kissing crust as from a warden pie', I got behind Liz. The Beadle told us that her ghost still walked there. I was no Black Prince.

On the way home I asked Liz what was a warden pie? Hard little green pears, she said, Kentish wardens. In the potting-shed next day I questioned Henry about ghosts. Were there any ghosts? I hadn't slept too well. There was a wickerwork arm-chair in my room, it creaked sometimes, with a noise like a sigh; shivery, if you were awake. We were planting the winter frames with Marie Louise double violets, sitting on the edge of the frame as we talked. Henry was cagey. He'd never seen one, but he wasn't prepared to say there were none. Anything was likely. He was diplomatic. He had known a Sikh in India who swore he'd met his brother on patrol on the N.W.F. and heard next day that he'd died in Simla a week before. But, there, India was a long way away, hundreds of miles. It wasn't at all the sort of thing for little girls to worry about. I agreed, and we left it like that. A few days later the basket chair went down to the maids' sitting-room.

Through Henry's eyes I saw history as a living study; not a collection of disjointed facts, but as a broad highway which we all tread as part of an eternal, continuing purpose. Where all time, past, present and future, are one. Where nothing can happen that has never happened before, and nothing can ever happen again, because people are people. Human nature is the eternal constant, unchanging. That was a tremendous concept to hand on to a child without scaring the living daylights out of her.

It wasn't always history that took us to Dover. We used to make one or two excursions every spring to get samphire for Authority's favourite pickle. We would drive as far as Ashford in the trap, leave it at the mews and with picnic basket and sacks for the herb we caught the train. Samphire grew in considerable quantities in the rocks below the old castle. A strange, bony-looking plant, dusty bluish-green in colour, of a strong, hottish salty taste, with a sharp aromatic pungence, reminiscent of cough mixture, fennel and chrysanthemums. It grew in cracks and rock crannies where anything else would have starved. It was perennial. We cut it when it was about four inches high, still in close spikes, and tender. Liz sat knitting whilst I drowsed at her knees, watching Henry climbing like a Gibraltar monkey, filling his sack.

When he'd got sufficient, he'd come and sit with us, smoke a pipe of 'bacca', and tell of the old seamen who used to come ashore in spring to cut samphire to cure scurvy, after long winter voyaging on salt meat and hard biscuit, their skin dry and

SAMPHIRE
CRISTE MARINE

Herbe d'Saint Pierre. St Peter of the Rocks. Samphire. Known to Seafarers for centuries as an anti-scorbutic, with a coastal distribution throughout the Northern Hemisphere. It was the first growing plant to start growth in the spring, in crevices of rocks and on beaches. Eagerly gathered and eaten raw—or pickled—after long periods on salt meat and hard tack.

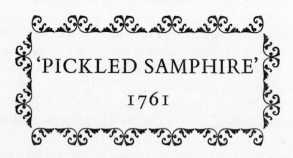

'PICKLED SAMPHIRE'
1761

Take shoots of Samphire new sprung. Lay it in a pan, with two or three handfuls of salt. Cover with fresh spring water. Let stand a day and a night. Then put all into a Brass Saucepan, cover close. Set over a very slow fire and let stand until the Herbe is green and crisp. Remove from heat at once, for if it become the least boiled or soft, it be spoiled.

Place the whole in Stone Jars, in layers. When quite cold, cover with fresh Vinegar. Cover with bladders and tie well down.

N.B. Bladder was Pig's Bladder. Could be bought at the Butchers, cleaned, dried and kept for use.

harsh and vitality at a low ebb. Holy herb of Saint Peter, for hundreds of years celebrated as an anti-scorbutic, samphire of the rocks is the first green thing to start into growth in spring.

After we had eaten our tea, Liz would fill the hamper with sea spinach, and we were ready to catch the train back to Ashford.

The pickling of samphire required fresh spring water, so did many other recipes. This was always fetched by Cookie, who trusted no one but herself to do the job. There must be no grit scooped from the spring, no foreign bodies.

Water for the house was pumped by the garden boys into vast roof tanks, at a two-handled pump in the yard. It was called the engine, for some obscure reason. Cookie didn't trust this well water, except for scrubbing and baths. She took her great oaken buckets out through the nut-walk, where, in the bottom of a sloping meadow beyond the orchard, there was a lovely spring. It nestled in the hollow of what had once been a gravel pit and ran away through the grass. From the orchard level a fairly steep-sloping path led down to the water. A dipper hung on a stump beside the spring. Generations of country-women had worn a pretty slidy path down to the bottom. In dry weather one could slide down on a board; great fun. If you leaned right at the bottom you landed in the water. If you leaned left you capsized and continued down to the bottom of the slope. On early, dewy mornings it was a dicey descent, and was poor Cookie's downfall.

Her two big buckets, sacred to fresh spring water, were coopered with three iron bands. One early morning she parked one bucket at the top of the slope and started down. Mrs Havinden had been before her and spilt half her load coming up the path. Cookie slipped, and landed in the spring, sitting in the bucket where she stuck like a cork in a bung-hole. Her beam was wide; struggle as she might she could not free herself. Her seat stuck tighter as her skirts got wetter. She shouted for help, but no one heard her. Struggling hard, she managed to roll on to hands and knees but was worse off than before. She kept calling for help and at last a farmhand, passing along the lane beyond the spring field, heard her, and pushing through the hedge tried to kick the bucket off. He said as 'e reckoned 'the bucket was stuck'. She implored him to find Henry.

Henry said afterwards that when he caught sight of her she looked like a mangabey monkey with his rump up. He and Billy Bennett split off the two top coopered bands and she was free, a very upset and ruffled Cookie. It was to Henry's eternal credit that he kept a straight face all the way back to the kitchen with Cookie on his arm and, teetotaller or not, forced her to take a brandy.

Afterwards in the Bothy, he laughed until the tears ran down his face. Billy Bennett took a load of timber to the meadow, and thereafter a flight of steps and a handrail spoilt the slide. 'Good/ness!' said Mrs Havinden. 'Why didn't nobody think of it before; me going for water sometimes three times a day, in all weathers and never falling down yet.'

CHAPTER FOUR

If Authority was at home, his birthday in July was celebrated by a garden party and a house full of guests, with fireworks, and an estate party-treat for all on the vicarage glebe.

I didn't like house parties. People drifting all over the place and helping themselves to our peaches. They were friends, yes, but they would insist on kissing me. I was pretty choosy about kissing. They got in my way. I hated the way the womenfolk fluffed around Henry, coaxing buttonholes of our choicest flowers out of him. I suppose I was jealous as a cat. Henry was mine, and to see him knocking up a 'corsage piece' to match a fashionable dress made me green. I laugh now at the little beast I must have been.

One or two ladies brought their personal maids along to dress them like dollies. They always breakfasted in bed and didn't face the menfolk until lunchtime. Trays, trays, trays. An endless procession of coffee-pots and a really furious Cookie in a smoking paddy. She hated 'em too, but for another reason. The ladies' maids were always demanding a hot iron to smooth creases out of silks, or rainwater to wash laces. She gave them short shrift, hunting them across the yard to the laundry room. Said Cookie, 'They're all ears and gossip—and eyes. They can stay out of my kitchen! Good recipes are saleable in London.' And good cook's recipes were her secret; her stock-in-trade, as it were. She guarded them. Cookie's great leather-bound recipe book had a lock and key. In that book there was a sheet of brown paper and a piece of glass. When the book was open on the kitchen table the glass protected the page and the brown paper foxed all peepers. When it was closed, and locked, the key hung from Cookie's waist-belt.

She had good reason to be suspicious of these smart maids. Cookie was an expert in many sides of housewifery. Her toilet-water was the best I've ever come across. Light, sweet and mysterious. Oh, yes, recipes were saleable. One French maid, Celestine, had sneaked into the still-room on the q.t. one afternoon and pinched Cookie's recipe for 'Breath of Cytherea', selling it afterwards to a small-time perfumer in Paris. It wasn't much good to him because she had got her quantities mixed up and he wanted his money back. She got the sack for that. She was a bad baggage, said Liz, who, I afterwards found out, hated her just as I did. Old Mrs Dence said she was a man-trap, and was chasing Henry. Henry got the jitters. She had a nasty habit of oiling into the shed and calling 'Hon-ree! Hon-ree!', giggling and bridling like a parakeet. When we heard her calling, Henry would go at the double for the palace of ease behind the Bothy and lock himself in until the menace had taken herself off. Authority thought it was terribly funny, so did my Godfather. I didn't. I used to put out my tongue at her, and

SPRING FLOWERS

Cookie's
Toilet Water
1723

SPIRITS OF WINE I *pint*

ESSENCE OF VIOLETS $\frac{1}{2}$ *ounce*

SPIRITS OF ROSEMARY $\frac{1}{2}$ *ounce*

ESSENCE OF BERGAMOT $\frac{1}{2}$ *a drachm*

OIL OF VERBENA $\frac{1}{2}$ *a drachm*

ESSENCE OF JASMINE $\frac{1}{2}$ *a drachm*

OIL OF LAVENDER $\frac{1}{4}$ *a drachm*

ORANGE FLOWER WATER $\frac{1}{2}$ *ounce*

ROSEWATER $\frac{1}{4}$ *pint*

Mix and filter through blotting paper.
Bottle for the toilet.

that was an awful thing to do. No lady ever stuck her tongue out, except for the doctor. She complained to Liz, and Liz threatened to spank me. I don't think she meant it.

Heigh ho! We were glad when the visit ended, and Henry said, 'Thank God.' He reckoned that Eve must have been a French-woman.

If Authority was away on duty, his birthday was celebrated by the whole estate; a trip to the sea and a day out. My God-father came to stay for a while and help Henry with business matters, and on the date a break from Cranbrook Mews was at the drive gate by nine a.m. The wagonette, loaded with pro-visions and drinks, was already ahead, Cookie, Liz and God-father on board, with Havinden on the box, his oppo. Jack Dence. Henry skippered the break and Mrs Havinden duen-na-ed the women and children. I rode with Henry on the outward journey, with Liz on the way home, mostly fast asleep on the floor of the wagonette.

The horsedrawn break was the forerunner of the chara' and the motor-coach. Two or four horses pulled what is best described as a four-wheeled, high, wooden toast-rack, a double row of seats facing ahead, two passengers to each seat, with a centre gangway reached by a short collapsible ladder at the rear. A double rail all round kept passengers from falling on to the highway. The wheels were iron-tyred; the noise on stone-metalled roads appalling. There was no overhead cover. On dry days you choked with dust. If it came on to rain, you got wet. It was as simple as that. Nobody minded. A day out was a day out; you took what the gods dished out to you, and liked it. Springing was sketchy. On a long drive the wooden seats were purgatorial perches. The best of cushioned bottoms re-belled; the thin ones, well, just imagine it if you can! Old hands brought along 'summat t' set on. Tes 'ard on the backside, like.'

The driver sat, godlike, high on the box, Henry beside him, myself between them, a strap about my waist, shackled to the seat. I was known to be fidgety. The horses' nosebags were slung below the back rail, whilst the hopper sat behind, with his legs dangling over the folded step-ladder. His job was to hop off on the steep down gradients and fix the steel shoe-drags under the back wheels to brake the speed. Oh, the rasping noise of these! His most important job was, well, most important. When passing nicely-wooded scenery it was he who decided when the ladies might like to 'stretch their legs and visit Mrs Murphy'. He never waited until some child yelled, 'Hi! Stop, mister! Willie Maxted wants to pee!' He wasn't a family man: but he seemed to know. His was a most responsible position.

People in this day and age, who know only cradling springs and sponge-rubber comfort, cannot possibly imagine what a day out was like before the turn of the century. The fun we had. No tarmac smoothness, no Rolls Royce coachwork, no rubber tyres. Yet anticipation, realisation and celebration were every-thing. On boarding the break each child was given a shilling to spend on a bucket and spade. For their mothers it was a day of peace and absolute relaxation, of neighbourly gossip and friendship.

The last person to come on the scene was Farmer Harvey, with two huge rick covers. He was a pessimist. 'Y'never know, might rain.' They were stowed under the back seat, and he waved us off. Nine-thirty was deadline. As we got rolling, Henry started the seaside song; everybody knew the tune.

> 'Down by the sea, down by the sea,
> We'll have a lively time, you bet, down by the sea.
> Trunks and boxes all upset,
> Fifty kids and a bassinet,
> We'll have a lively time, you bet, down by the sea.'
> Etc., etc.

We all sang. Old Mrs Dence, who couldn't sing at all, did her best; and Mrs Havinden, who was inclined to be a bit stiff as befitted the wife of a head keeper, sang as well, albeit refinedly.

❧ IMPERIAL POP ☙

Into a large glazed earthen vessel put—

3 ozs of Cream of Tartar

1½ lbs of White Sugar

The bruised peel and juice of two Lemons

1 oz of Root Ginger—well bruised

Boil 1½ gallons of Fresh Spring Water, and cool to blood heat.
Add to the ingredients in the vessel, with 1 oz of Yeast.
Stir well several times.
Cover and stand overnight, well covered, then strain and bottle it.
Tie corks tight.

THIS MAKES A COOLING DRINK IN HOT
WEATHER, OR IN THE SICK ROOM.

In these times the polythene bucket replaces all the old-time earthenware utensils.
Why on earth need mothers pay ten new pence for a bottle of fizzy drink for the youngsters when they can make a couple of gallons for very little more? No mess—no fuss—and the simplest of ingredients·

You see, there was hierarchy even amongst the workers in those days. Protocol descended, class defended.

The amount of forethought, indoor effort, and staff work the day out entailed was terrific. Cookie and Liz, with the maids, were busy as bees. Mrs Dence and Mrs Havinden came in to lend willing hands. Such a baking of pies, chicken pies, pork pies, steak pies, fruit pies, take your pick, luscious inside, lovely pastry, nothing spared. Individual packs of chicken and ham, cold sausages and pickled walnuts; dozens and dozens of hard-boiled eggs, devilled drumsticks and gooseberry chutney.

Slabs of caraway seed cake; this was for menfolk, they loved it. It seems to have gone out of fashion today—time was when a glass of madeira wine and a slice of caraway cake was the regular country elevenses. There was cut-and-come-again cake, stiff with plummy raisins and cherries, and lemon buns. Cheddar and Stilton cheese in ripe, tasty lumps. Zinc buckets of radishes and land-cress and crisp 'cos' lettuce, with baskets of fresh, crusty bread and butter. It was all there. Not forgetting a basketful of china mugs.

Cookie really put her heart into the job. To wet dry whistles there were gallon jars of orange cider, imperial pop for the small fry and quantities of cool tankard for the grown-ups. Cool tankard was a cold punch: only one of the many things stored away in her Aladdin's cave of delightful recipes. It is strange that a staunch blue ribbonist never saw anything incongruous in all this drink, but there it was, it was picnic fare.

Our picnic days were long remembered. Excepting for one experimental flop, we went to Whitstable, where the shops were all handy, the beach safe, sandy and soft to sit upon. Here we knew all the ropes. Godfather made a beeline for a snug little bar he knew, where he'd leisurely swallow a couple of dozen natives—oysters, of course—with a half-pint of chablis, before settling down to sleep on the sand with *The Times* over his head until lunchtime, when he came to life to organise the cricket match, and to hit such terrific boundaries that the kids were run off their legs. Their mothers ransacked the shops before teatime. My chief recollection of Whitstable is of straw-hatted young men in extraordinary striped blazers, eating whelks and cockles at the sea-front stalls in an atmosphere thick with the fumes of vinegar. They appeared to relish these strange delicacies. I tried a whelk once. I couldn't do anything with it. I tried chewing. Half an hour later I was still chewing. Liz caught me and said, 'Spit that out, at once!' I spat. It went quite a long way. What was the lure of the seaside whelk stall? Do they still eat whelks in July at Whitstable?

We couldn't have done it all without Henry. He dug great tunnels and holes in the sand, made pies in buckets, sand-castles and devices. He turned skipping-ropes, tied up grazed knees, played cricket. A veritable tower of strength. At the end of the day it was he who winkled the dads out of the pub, soothed anxious mums who hadn't seen their offspring since teatime, piggy-backed weary children to the break, with pear-drops, yellow or red, to silence squallers. They were never ready to leave for home. At the drive gate all sang the children's hymn, 'Now the day is over, night is drawing nigh.' 'Three cheers for the Boss. Hip, hip, hip . . .' and another bead slipped on the necklace of memory.

Our one and only experimental day out had been to Folke-stone. It was nearly a write-off. We were confronted by a steep, pebbled beach that promised no comfort to already stiffened posteriors. The ladies were unanimous, they weren't pleased. It wasn't up to much. The tide was rising and there was no sand. A forsaken spot if ever there was one. No fun.

After we had all been up in the lift to the Leas and down again, we'd seen the lot or so we thought, but we were wrong. The promenade was wet, spray was blowing off the shingles, but there was magic afoot. Godfather and Henry strolled off to see what might save a bad situation. There they were, at the harbour end of the promenade, in stitches of laughter; the children swarmed to see what it was all about. Henry had discovered the hens, laying hens! Godfather sent him to the bank in Tontine Street for ten shillings' worth of pennies, with the proviso that they had to be new pennies, to match the morning's magic. At intervals along the promenade, each hen, coloured as no living hen ever was, sat atop a green iron column waiting and willing to lay eggs for all comers, new-laid, tin eggs, containing half a dozen comfits. Mechanical hens they were. Push in a penny at her capacious breast end, hold a hand under her tail, wait whilst she wheezed a few metallic clucks, and eureka! there it was, right in your palm. Old Mrs Dence was fascinated. 'Couldn' espect t' get a newer laid then tha', could e'? Trouble was, you couldn' boil 'em.'

Quite a few hens had gone off lay before we ran out of pennies, then the fun was over with still most of the day to get through. Godfather said we'd drive inland to the downs and eat our lunch before going for a long drive, stopping for tea when we felt like it.

We pulled up at Fordwich, where Mrs Finch, whose husband was stockman at Harvey's Farm, volunteered to try the ducking stool. That made the party cackle a bit; Finch was rumoured to be a hen-pecked husband. With her petticoats ballooning so that all could see her long flannelette drawers, she was winched up and lowered perilously down over the River Stour. Entering into the fun of the occasion she screeched for mercy. Her twins caught the panic and screamed as well, attacking the winchman tooth and claw. Henry took them round to the bar and comforted them with home-made treacle toffee.

Earlier than usual, we started homewards. It hadn't been a lost day. 'But . . . well . . . you know, sir! . . . You can get free of the kids on the sand, see? No . . . no, sir! I ain't complaining. Whitstable's better, that's all.' Whitstable for ever!

Henry had a nice tenor voice, and sometimes when he felt carefree and we were driving through quiet lanes, he'd start a song. If Godfather was with us, he'd join in.

One day, after a shopping spree in Maidstone, Godfather was whistling *The Cavalry Canter*, occasionally tickling the cob's ears with the whip, at peace with the world and all men, driving along at a spanking pace. Henry started *The Road to Mandalay* and we all piped up.

Rounding a corner, short of Cranbrook, we were almost atop two travelling tinkers, fighting like tomcats in the dusty lane. A big bullock of a man and a wizened little fellow half his size, and the little chap was losing. Each time the big man landed a punch, a woman squatting on the roadside bank cheered. Godfather reined in smartly, stopping alongside, but they didn't seem to notice. Godfather said, 'There's murder afoot. Break it up, Henry.'

It was a job right up Henry's street; he had boxed for the regiment. He was out of the trap in a jiffy. Skipping up to the big tinker he hauled him off a lemon, knocking him sideways. Released, the little man vanished through the hedge. The bully rolled sideways on to his feet in one skilful move; sizing up Henry, he let out a yell, and arms flailing sailed in to attack. Henry waited just long enough before letting him have a straight right and left. Both landed, whump! Flat as a dab, the bully was out cold. The woman stared in unbelief, sprang up, rushed at Henry and landed a smacking kiss on his face, then flung herself on the vanquished hero. Taking him by the hair, she started banging his head, right heartily, in the dust.

Godfather threw her half-a-crown. She stopped banging just long enough to push it down her stays, before starting again. I was only a little girl and didn't fully comprehend what it was all about, but, oh, it was funny—truly funny—and I laughed myself sick.

A few weeks later the big tinker drove into our kitchen yard seeking pots to mend. He was alone. Henry was at the pump. The tinker didn't wait, he whipped up his pony and was off down the back drive like Jehu.

We knew that the woman was no longer with him. It had been a casual affair, more than a little stormy. After settling her scores with the man in the lane, she'd emptied his pockets and skipped off, leaving him unconscious. The law had picked him up and given him a few nights' free lodging in the work-house. We had all this gossip from our local constable, P.C. Cornford, colloquially, P.C. Jellybelly. Jolly, red-faced, stout almost to discomfort, it was a blessing that the countryfolk were a law-abiding lot. Too fat to run, he couldn't have arrested a tortoise. He patrolled his beat on a bike, all the countryside between Cranbrook and Staplehurst. Heat or frost, wet or fine, he rode up our drive twice a day for a cup of 'summat hot' with Cookie. He knew all that went on. He was a bit dim at times, but reliable.

There was a story that, in his very early days in the force, young and on his mettle, anxious to show what a good copper he was, he had been passing the Cricketers' Arms when a gipsy had been nabbed whilst robbing the till. Forbidden by regulations to leave his bike, he had solved his dilemma by handcuffing his captive to the bike and starting for the lock-up on foot. Twenty minutes later he was in the ditch, bike and captive missing.

P.C. Cornford was a flop. He never picked up any pro-motion, just got fatter, more human, loved and trusted by all. If there were a few local peccadilloes, they were settled quietly. What use to make a fuss when you had to go miles for a copper? Settle things quietly. Sleep on it; and as Cookie always de-clared, 'Best bake your pie in your own oven.' D.T.s, wife-beatings and hop-pickers gave him the most trouble. But there, hop-pickers were city folks. Their ways were different. So P.C. Jellybelly watched over us all, winter and summer.

(43)

CHAPTER FIVE

Summer was flower-show time. To watch Henry preparing for an exhibition was to see endless patience and precision, concluding long months of team-work and preparation. Nothing less than absolute perfection satisfied him. Everything for staging, excepting sweet peas, was cut overnight. Sweet peas were left until sunrise on the day, after heavy watering so they were full of moisture.

With the treasures gathered into the shed we watched Henry stroking and coaxing unruly petals into perfect alignment, sometimes nipping an ugly one out altogether, with such absolute expertise, you'd never guess there had ever been a petal at all; a wizard, with ivory tweezers and camel-hair brushes, his touch light as a feather. Soft loops of white Berlin wool were tied around rosebuds so that they couldn't spring before being placed in the boards. It was not customary then to show roses in vases; they were cut short, not more than two leaves on the stems, and placed facing upwards in perforated boards so that the exquisite blooms might be fully appreciated. Perfection of shape brought marks.

Carnations and picotees, pansies and violas were also shown like this, and I must say they looked very lovely. It took the very nicest judgment to decide which of our carnations might prove to be a 'buster' before the judges got round the benches. Not for Henry the aid of a split ring, pushed up under the petals. Henry always declared that plunging cut flowers made them lose texture under marquee conditions. Keep them in the dark, stage early, leaving them to drink. His recipe for that drink was rainwater, half a gallon, two tablespoons of sugar and three bottles of Mumby's soda water. This secret weapon was mixed in the water cans and taken with us.

I can recommend the soda water treatment for all cut flowers, especially for carnations, which will keep much longer after purchase.

Really star shows for me were those when Henry chose to create a wedding bouquet, for exhibition only. The artist went to work. His bouquets for any occasion were really lovely; lucky the bride amongst our friends who could coax Henry to do her wedding flowers. These were terrific occasions. He was driven to Ashford junction before daylight, with wicker dress-baskets full of flowers, attended by Jack Dence and a couple of promising garden lads. They loved the excitement. The bouquets went along in large hat-boxes, packed into the guard's van. Henry went with his precious cargo in the van.

In those faraway days, wedding bouquets were confections, like hats and gowns. They epitomised the romanticism and sentimental outlook of the period. Delicate trails of smilax and asparagus *plumosus* rippling down to the hems of silken petticoats. Noble fistfuls of blossoms, bound with streamers of satin ribbons. Yet there was no suggestion of heaviness. Five small arums or Harrisi lilies, three carnations, nine blooms of stephan/otis or lily of the valley sprays. Two rosebuds for good measure, with maidenhair fronds to balance the whole; light and airy, complementing the fashions of the day. Frills and flounces, tight bodices and swirling skirts to the feet; six/yard trains, lined with ruched Valenciennes lace or chiffon; veils of ancestral old lace, or yards and yards of white tulle veiling. All a question of the *coup d'oeil*. 'The eyeful,' said Henry: and they were.

A perfect bouquet was a whole afternoon's work. When all preparations for the show were complete and packed into the wagonette ready for an early start, we were away to our beds. I couldn't sleep for hours. I was already savouring the delights of the marquees, magical, dim caverns of grey/green twilight, where footsteps were muted by grass underfoot; delightful, with the for/ever/to/be/remembered exquisite atmosphere, most cherished recollection of childhood. Mingled perfumes of Dickson and Madame Abel Chatenay roses, blood/red and silken pink; stocks and clove carnations; bergamot, and pep/pery, spicy phlox; sweet peas and ripe strawberries, lemon verbena; crushed celery leaves; green onions; shag 'bacca' and trodden turf. All topped off with stray whiffs of Winche's Kentish Ale. Sheer essence of rural heaven.

So different from the sophistication of the afternoon, when Jockey Club, Russian Violet, Chypre, Carnation by Rimmel of Paris, and the flick of silk handkerchiefs releasing *eau/de/Cologne*, clogged the natural scents; and the frou/frou of taffeta petticoats replaced the jolly, squeaky rubbing of new corduroy trousers, which made the morning bustle so very bustling. Morning. Camaraderie, fun and discreet hurry. Exhibitors milling and dodging, apologising. 'Whoa there! . . . sorry, mate! . . . didn't see you there. It's this darn great pot plant! . . . No harm done! . . . Want any help?' Warmth and friendship. Somebody, usually a lady, wailing she'd lost her scissors. Could someone lend a pair for a minute? Bless 'em, they all knew Henry carried a spare pair.

Generous, but canny, the only thing Henry never lent—unless it was quite empty—was a watering-pot. You don't make competitors as wise as yourself, was Henry's motto.

There were always the late-comers, well loaded, staggering into the guy-ropes, having to be helped to pick up the spillage, and make a start at the bench. I used to feel so proud of Henry on these occasions. He didn't forget anything and didn't flap; he was at his professional best. Preliminaries behind him, Jack to help him, everything ready, it was a military operation. Staging over, spares and replacements under the bench, and he was ready to lend a hand wherever needed.

The ladies loved him. He could be relied upon for a bit of fern or a spare bud to finish a table decoration. The village children waited eagerly for him to notice their wild flower exhibits, or their little peepshows.

These were fascinating little efforts; they are called 'flower designs' today. Their old use is forgotten long ago. The peep-show was a shallow box about nine inches square and three inches deep—Borwick's Packeted Baking Powder boxes were ideal. They enclosed intricate patterns of moss and petals and wee flowers, looking like cuttings of Persian carpeting; this was the peep. It was protected over the top by a sheet of glass, covered with strong brown paper. The whole constituted a peepshow: colloquially, a poppyshow. To raise the paper and look at the peep one paid a forfeit; a safety pin, a bit of treacle toffee, maybe a coveted blue bead off a fairground necklace, or just a striped alley marble.

The accosting formula was standardised: 'A pin to see the poppyshow, lady, please.' If you came across a tightfister who knew what she wanted, she'd beat the price up. Country kids weren't slow. Authority always provided himself with a couple of dozen threepenny bits; it was expected of him.

(48)

Henry used to encourage the garden boys to grow something to exhibit for themselves; and once, but never again, Bob Maxted chose to grow a vegetable marrow. A long, green one; it was to be the biggest marrow ever. There was no reason why it shouldn't be, said Henry, with everything that grew fat marrows ready to hand, rich earth, plenty of manure and practical know-how.

Bob chose a spot on the sunny side of the Bothy, where the rainwater from the roof was nice and handy. He dug a deepish hole and filled it with chopped stinging nettles to raise a great heat, stamped them well down, and built up his marrow bed. So far, so good. When the heat was right he sowed three seeds straight into the ground. They sprouted well. The slugs had one, the mice took number two, but the third flourished mightily. In due course there was a nice baby marrow. Bob drooled over his marrow. It was over nine inches long, he said; prospects of that first prize dazed his common-sense.

One Sunday afternoon he brought his girl friend, Aggie, to see his hopeful. Her father also grew prize marrows. It was easy, said Cookie, to see where he'd got the idea. Aggie allowed that it was a promising start and reckoned he was pretty clever. His pride was great. In a maze he left her, sitting beside the marrow, whilst he fetched her a cabbage leaf full of early strawberries. When she had eaten them, and buried the cabbage leaf for luck, they sauntered off to her home for Sunday tea, Bob moony over Aggie. As the show date got closer, the marrow grew bigger, fed with sugar water by a piece of worsted threaded through the stem from a container kept replenished. Aggie came several times to see its progress.

Heigh ho! Bob and she had a slanging match, and she didn't come again. Romance withered as the marrow waxed. The show date was on us. Late for every job he had to do, Bob made a dash to cut his marrow. Consumed only by a desire to beat Aggie's dad, he didn't turn it over to make sure it was clean. A very king of marrows, it lay on the show bench to beat all comers. The judges were unanimous—it was all it looked, and unblemished. Bob didn't beat Aggie's dad. Up-ended by the judges, there, for all to see, was the pin-scrawled message, 'AGGIE LOVES BOB'. She'd pin-scratched that message on the underside of Bob's baby marrow, whilst he was gone for the strawberries. It had grown with the marrow. Aggie's dad laughed.

Henry usually made a quick tour of the benches before the tents were cleared for judging. On the way to lunch he'd size up everybody's chances pretty shrewdly. A quick stand-up lunch, and even quicker change. The supreme moment was here. The dog-cart at the door; myself in starched, white broderie anglaise, wide taffeta sash and matching hair ribbons, with my parasol, and a white leghorn hat trimmed with a wreath of buttercups and daisies, stepping it out proudly between Authority and Henry. A most presentable and un-usual Henry, in a stiff collar that scrubbed his neck and made him swear, a rich crimson silk tie, with his gold horseshoe tiepin, a matching silk peeping from the breast pocket of his best slate-blue suit, his white linen 'blower' pushed up his sleeve. Under a doggy Trilby hat, set at just the right angle, his moustache was waxed into two imperial points. No clay cutty pipe today, his best briar, no less.

Authority always looked me over, and said, 'My dear, how nice you look today.' He was always gallant. I had nothing left to ask for. The two finest people in the world were escorting me. We were on our way.

Authority had the reins. Tapper's hoofs were clipping the highway, his harness jingling. My cup was full. There, at last, was the show-ground. The marquees, bunting and flags every-where. The bandstand. The band. The uniforms. The band-master. All the chairs. People arriving. On these occasions I was not lifted from the vehicle, I was handed down. I could unfurl my parasol with an air—I copied that off my Godfather's lady-friend. Life was a full basket. True, Liz and Cookie would arrive and collect me at half past four from my seat under the bandmaster's eye, but until then I savoured a grown-up world.

With the opening ceremonies over, and backslapping done, the strains of *The Gladiators* coming from the band, there was a sense of release and festivity. Authority always made the rounds of the marquees with us, and after congratulating Henry would press half a sovereign into his hand, bidding him do the honours amongst his craft brethren, tenants and nurserymen, tell me to be a good child and not be a nuisance to Henry, before dodging the Vicar's wife, who always made a bee-line for him in public. He was a handsome escort and she clung like burrs to a blanket. He would oil away to a small canvas tent, in a secluded position, until the coast was clear.

I loved the Vicar, an elderly, gentle, scholarly man, who asked nothing better than his studies in Babylonian history and to do his Christian duty in the parish. His silvery hair blew up round his head like a halo, his face was pink and cherubic, in his surplice he looked like a chubby Botticelli angel. He generally drifted round the benches, before finding a seat beside the bandstand and sleeping like a baby until his wife wanted to go home. I didn't care overmuch for her, and I suspected that was mutual.

A large woman, she bulged fore and aft like a Dutch doll. She smelled of stale violet powder and had a mauve nose, the smallest waist I have ever seen, which may have been the reason for that, and her stays creaked when she breathed. To stop and talk to her was like standing under a big tree on a windy day.

We had a kitchen maid once, who had worked at the vicarage. I overheard her telling Mrs Havinden that 'the old gent was a dear, but the old girl was a terror, so proud of her figure that she slept in her corset. There! What about that? Beats cockfighting, don't it? 'Tis true.'

I mulled this scrap of information over to myself. I was

worried. I'd seen Cookie's whalebone scaffolding drying on the clothes-line on washdays. How on earth could it be true? I asked my Godfather. A bachelor, with lots of friends in Paris; he ought to know. Cookie called him 'a bit of a blade.' He was no help. He laughed so much that he swallowed a cherry-stone and said, 'Why not ask the Vicar? Anyway, true or not, she certainly has a fine carriage.' But I knew she only drove a pony-chaise. I was more puzzled than ever.

I sought out Henry to get his opinion. I told him what Godfather had said. He laughed so much that he couldn't reply, then said women were daft and he couldn't say. Just forget it because it could never be proved. We left it like that, but I couldn't forget it. I used to walk all round her trying to solve the problem. The mystery was profound.

Left to ourselves at the show Henry and I made a critical assessment of all the exhibits. To me, this was tremendous pleasure. He was popular, had many contacts. There was much chat; listening carefully, I stored everything away in my mind to mull over in my bed that night.

Henry extracted information on methods and technical details with the expertise of a treecreeper hunting spiders in oak bark. I came off pretty well on these rounds. Quite a few choice spares came my way from underbench caches. Everybody knew Henry's Blister. A few hairy gooseberries; a couple of Reine Claude greengages, golden-green and perfumed; a ripe peach. All grist to a child who had been too excited to eat a decent lunch.

Chat and greetings over, all repaired to the buffet tent, meeting nurserymen and the favoured few not seen since the last big shows. The half sovereign was split in a magnificent gesture. Little girls were seen and not heard. I sat quiet with a small stone ginger, ears well back. Authority would come in to be sure I wasn't in the way, drink a beer and go his way. It was all so peacefully right, so unchanging. I was as good as gold. Happy. Yet, one day, I did blot my copybook; a day so hot and muggy that exhibits and exhibitors wilted together, when spectators felt all in and tightly-laced ladies fainted whole-sale and had to be revived with smelling-salts and toilet vinegar from their reticule bags. The bandsmen shed their uniform tunics and played on heroically in shirtsleeves and braces—a thing unheard of. The gentlemen puffed criticism. Shocking, quite unmentionably shocking! With the ladies around too, they clucked like ganders. 'What are we coming to?' Puff. Puff. Puff.

The tougher ladies clung to their chairs. They weren't too fussy, it was just heaven to sit down. There wasn't a breath of air. It got hotter and hotter. Westwards, in a brassy blue sky, dirty grey clouds like fat sheep were gathering, with faraway rumbles of thunder. Ladies were leaving. In the buffet, the atmosphere got thicker. Beer and 'bacca'. Phew! I'd eaten a good few oddments. Excitement, gooseberries, brandysnaps and ginger beer were at odds and began to rumble round.

The moment of decision was upon me. I announced, firmly, 'I'm going to be sick.' On the instant conversation died. They all stared. Bang on in every emergency, Henry said, 'Oh! You Blister,' whisked me out of decent company and fairly ran me round behind the buffet tent into a canvas convenience. He apologised and a startled gent withdrew in a hurry. Placing a firm hand across my middle and the other across my forehead, he bent me double, pressed me firmly and said, 'Spill.' I obeyed, thankfully.

'Have you finished?' I nodded gratefully. Without more ado he mopped my chin with a clean handkerchief, straightened my hat and strolled me back to my seat, fetched me a soda-water and finished his beer.

Somebody said, 'Well! As I said before we got interrupted.' I was only a minnow in a big pond. I drank my soda water and waited for Henry to take me out to the bandstand to wait for Liz and Cookie. When they came I was fast asleep.

The day after each show we tacked all the prize cards up on

the Bothy walls beside all the lovely coloured flower-plates presented weekly by the *Gardeners Chronicle*, Queen Victoria looking down on everything from her place of honour above the stove. A quaint, disapproving little face, her hair parted above her nose in two smooth plasters. Her fan clasped in jewelled fingers, a white lace shawl draped over her head. She presided over *Bubbles* and *The Old Folks at Home* and the famous *Blue Boy*, all Pears' annual supplements. I loved all the coloured flower-plates; with their help I learned my alphabet. A for Abelia. B for Bongardia. C for Calendula. The names chimed like bells. I could sing them to music of my own making and learn faster. Much more fun, more comprehensible than the old jingle, 'A was an archer who shot at a frog.' Who'd shoot frogs, anyhow? Daft! I was proud of the showcards and all they represented. The team work. They were testimony to 'us', but the mind of a child is thistledown, a weathercock, blown hither and thither, without rhyme or reason.

So it fell out that in spite of all my pride I once dashed Henry's hopes of a county first for potatoes. For some reason that was important, Henry was away on a message for Authority. Liz was busy, Cookie locked in the still-room making liqueurs. At a loose end, I was mooching all over the place on no particular ploy. As I passed through 'smother corner', there was a lovely stinking bonfire going, at the base a glowing cavern, just right for baking potatoes. Ah! that would fill the time nicely. To think was to do.

The technique was simple. Toss your potatoes into a good hot spot, and squat on your heels until they looked done. Black as coal and mostly half raw on one side, they were ambrosial, lovely grub. I went hunting for stray potatoes. I could have gone to the kitchen, but it didn't pay to advertise. Eating between meals was naughty. I went to the potting-shed. Witless day. I didn't notice a basketful of potatoes just inside the door: on the bench lay eight. Seizing three I beetled off back to the fire with a head empty of all but one thought.

Tossing them into the cavern I squatted to watch them cook. They were just coming along to a nicety when there was a yelp of sheer anguish from the potting-shed, and the wrath of doom was upon me. My heart hit my brain-pan. Henry! A Henry transformed by his loss into a purple-faced demon of vengeance. He stared, incredulously, down at the potatoes. My potatoes, his potatoes, our potatoes, turning black in the heat. Then at me. I thought he was about to shake me. He didn't. In devastating silence he reached for a pitchfork standing against the wall, and thrust the apex of the bonfire right down over my plunder. Only when there was no possibility of rescue did he speak. His words were clods on my head. From his very heart they came. 'You—you Blister!' he yelled at me. 'Oh, you Blister! It wouldn't have mattered if you'd only taken two! Suffering cats, where's your sense? That's all you'll see of the show, my lady. The show! Oh, the show!' The full iniquity of what I'd done struck me like a brick. I'd forgotten the show and Henry had said no show for me. There could be no greater punishment. Without a second look Henry walked away. I heard the shed door slam and he took away the key.

In deepest shame and dejection I sought my private sanctuary, under the laurel hedge down the back drive, and abandoned myself to my misery. I was in deep disgrace. I wept. Life was flat, stale and unprofitable. Henry went straight from the potting-shed to the Cricketers' Arms, three miles away, to drown his disappointment and frustration, and he didn't return after closing time.

In the early dawn hours, Siddy the mailman, stopping his van to collect our mailbox from the lodge doorway, found him in the ditch, sleeping it off, his head in a clump of cow parsnip and his feet in six inches of muddy water. Siddy knocked up Havinden and together they got the soaker on to a hand-cart. Siddy went on his way with Her Majesty's mails whilst Havinden trundled his logged cargo to the stables and decanted him on to a heap of straw, pulled his sodden boots off, and covered him with a couple of horse-covers. It wasn't the first time. It wouldn't be the last. In after years I was to learn that this was the only expression of joy or sorrow Henry ever used, and to learn that, no matter how tight he got, he could steer a straight course, eyes front, the epitome of dignity and politesse—until he had to turn a corner. Then he was like a ship without a rudder. There was always the ditch outside the gate. Poor Henry.

I didn't see Henry for a fortnight. I was told not to ask questions. He was ill. Liz's eyes were red and the corner of her apron always wet. I thought I'd killed him. My stock was pretty low. Authority stalked the place with a face like thunder. I kept well out of the way, spending most of the time either under the laurels or pottering in the coverts. Life was empty of all interest, empty as a last year's crow's nest. The period ended, as all such did, with Liz going to the village shop for a box of Seidlitz powders, with Henry taking his big blue moustache mug and a spoon to the pump and swallowing four fizzers one after the other just as fast as he could swallow them. Next day he was back on the job: a mere shadow of himself.

Meeting him after lunch in the walled garden, I asked politely after his health. What had they given him to eat whilst he was ill? I thought only of beef tea and port-wine jelly. Jaunty as a cock sparrow, he said, off-hand, 'Oh! peach pudden and roasted peacocks.' And in proof of such marvels, he pulled two peacock's feathers from under his jacket—for me. I wasn't to know that he'd pinched them from the bar parlour at the Cricketers'. What a lovely invention to tell a child. The magic of childhood clung to Henry as scraps of eggshell cling to newly-hatched chicks. Magic walked with him; all round him. A pied piper. Spinner of the most enchanting fairy stories and animal tales.

In his hands chunks of firewood became whole families of wooden dollies with movable arms and legs. From half-ripe elder wood he made pan-pipes and pop-guns and pea-shooters.

He could get the most eldritch screeches from dandelion stalks, and at the snap of his fingers, pennies materialised out of the sky, off your hair-ribbons or out of pinafore pockets.

Looking back to those lovely days I can well believe that peach pudden and roast peacocks were the very substance of his dreams. We tacked the feathers behind the potting-shed door. Potatoes were never mentioned again. He sat me in the wheelbarrow with the tools, and gave me the tea-bottle to hold. I watched him tie on his apron. Paradise was open again.

CHAPTER SIX

Several months after the potato contretemps, Henry saved my
life. I was to accompany Authority to Maidstone, ordering trees
for November planting. Henry was to drive the dogcart. A
visit to old Mr Bunyard at the nurseries was a great treat. He
always treated me with a most delightful courtesy, calling me his
sweet little missie, which did a lot for my youthful vanity.
Awaiting me there was, invariably, a tiny toby jug of sweet
cider, two ginger nuts and a seat in the sun whilst business was
being discussed. How I loved it all.

Dressed for a visit, I was all ready to go. Liz had tricked me
out in my new pearl-grey pelisse, black velvet triple cape, collar
and cuffs. A bonnet to match, with black chin ties and two

black ostrich-feather pom-poms at the side. All children wore feather trimmings in those days, even baby boys. It was the thing. Even tiny baby bonnets had swans-down frills. Liz pulled on my white kid button boots, and gloves to match, before escorting me downstairs to the front porch to wait for the transport. In my black velvet dorothy bag I had a nice clean hanky and a wee purse containing fivepence. I was ready. Telling me to mind my p's and q's, daring me to stir foot or finger, she left me.

I wasn't used to sitting still for long. I fidgeted, opened my purse, counted my pennies, put them back, firmed the strings of my bag, opened it, and blew my nose, which was dry anyway. Time seemed endless. No dogcart. Oh dear! I eyed the lawn. There was surely no harm in stretching my legs. Why not? I couldn't get messed up on the grass, could I? I tiptoed across the gravel and pottered round, inspecting our formal bedding scheme. In pyrethrum, golden feather, darkest lobelias and silver-edging geranium, IND. IMP. VICT. REG. FID. DEF. were feeling the pull of a late summer season. Time they came out. So, too, the Imperial Crown. The central notion of obedience became blurred by a froth of inconsequent notions. I got bolder and left for the kitchen yard and my Waterloo.

In one corner of the yard a great barrel was sunk to half its depth in the ground. Henry called it the Tun. It caught the rainwater off the laundry roof, this being considered wonderful for ladies' complexions and the laundering of fine silks and laces. With the lid on, being banged with a stick, the barrel was a tom-tom, calling savage tribes to war; until Cookie came out like a wasp from a jam-jar and chased me away. Open, it was a target for stones. And here it was; the last user had not replaced the lid! Eureka! Hallelujah! My wits sent skating. I forgot I was a sweet little missie going visiting. I forgot my white kid gloves.

Scraping up a couple of handfuls of gravel, I let drive, getting a reasonable return. Yearning for greater results, I ferreted out half a brick and slung it in. Whoosh! It was a beauty. Looking to recover it for a second go, I leaned too far. With no time to scream, in I went. The sides of the Tun held me trapped, head down, unable to struggle. There, but for one blessed chance, I should have ended. Chance was Henry, cutting at the double for the front porch. Hearing the splash and thinking it might be the kitchen mouser, he turned into the yard to investigate.

He saw my little kid boots half-way down the barrel, the rest of me below the water. He hauled me out, held me up to drain and carting me to the front lawn began artificial respiration whilst Authority rode off to find the doctor. I was nearly a goner, said Henry. It was an hour before I came round. He refused to believe I wouldn't.

Liz immediately plunged me into a hot bath, dosed me with castor oil and rolled me in hot blankets until I sweated like a sausage. That was all a matter of routine; in the country-side you knew your first aid principles or died before the doctor arrived. Dose or die was the watchword, castor oil a noble standby. A rural doctor with a sprawling practice might be anywhere within a radius of ten miles, with all his apparatus in the box of his dogcart, or delivering a baby in some remote cottage across ploughed fields. The principles of domestic medicine were part and parcel of female education. Castor oil was thick, cluggy stuff; wouldn't leave the bottle, nor go down your throat, unless first made hot. A hot glass, a hot spoon, the bottle standing in boiling hot water, then proceed. A table-spoon of orange juice. A tablespoon of the oil. Another table-spoon of the juice and quick. Oopsy chin-chin! Down she goes. Queasy stomachs rejected it, pronto. I never got a chance. Liz held my nose. Swallow or choke; no choice but to swallow, but it was hard work keeping it down. My stomach churned. Half an hour later a big mugful of hot soup or tea. It went through you like dynamite. I was pretty tough. In a fortnight I was out and about, Blistering around again; but it taught me a lesson. I don't like water in masses, not even the sea. Phobia, maybe.

It was a nine days' wonder. I was drowned and resuscitated in the bar at the Cricketers', a dozen times. Authority presented Henry with a gold Albert and inscribed medallion, to match the watch he'd given him years before in India. That too had been for life-saving. Once more he had handled a crisis with knowledge and despatch.

Authority had once said of Henry that he was one of those born to walk safely in any street, to speak a common tongue, to approach, assess, and solve any situation, without fuss. Liz used to put it more simply. She said, 'Bless him! He's got a plaster for every corn.' He had. He was always on call for some trouble or other.

Authority had a soft spot for gipsies, which was a strange thing in a land-owner. They were free to camp on the clearing in the north covert, providing that they did not foul the spring in the small meadow, or cause damage and trouble: or the privilege would be withdrawn. They never did. He held that they were human beings, that they had a code of decency. Treated as such they behaved themselves well.

If they cut alder saplings for peg-making and thinned the hazel thickets for hurdles and faggots, they saved Havinden the job and kept us supplied with birch-besoms for sweeping the lawns. It cut both ways.

Keeper Havinden and his Oppo weren't so well disposed. They watched and spied around, yearning to catch a delinquent, wanting evidence. Havinden swore that they took pheasants and partridges, that the women set the children to pinch his cabbages and potatoes. The gipsy women smiled darkly. Following the discovery of a mass of mixed feathers blowing along a side, he strode with P.C. Jellybelly into the circle of caravans demanding that they should inspect the contents of the stewpot bubbling over the fire. His arrival was not unexpected. He wasn't the only one who kept a sharp look-out. The big lid was raised, willingly. All he saw was a rabbit stew, pepped up with gobbets of fresh grass-snake. Whilst P.C. Jellybelly rode off on his bike, Havinden was being sick behind the hedge—to the joy of the women. Nobody told him that because Imelda's baby was a bedwetter, his mother had emptied the sodden cot ticking into the wind. Why should they? They didn't like him.

To me the gipsies were a strange withdrawn race of people, the women secret and watchful. The men walked silently, like cats on the prowl. Friendly enough they seemed. They scared me.

Henry said that in the Cricketers' they were coolly sociable, making cheer that was of lip only, not of heart or eye, moody and quick-tempered; touchy was the word.

Authority said nonsense. They were a proud race who had been chased and persecuted, much as the Jews had been. They had acquired a protective covering. It had made them proud. The children were as shy as mice, rarely fraternising even with the East Enders at hopping time. Only the boys seemed to wish to leave camp.

The gipsy men spent days peeling the green alder rods for peg-making, cutting the prepared wood into lengths of six inches, before splitting and binding the unsplit two inches with narrow strips of soft tin, which the women cut from empty cocoa tins. Cookie saved all ours for the gipsies. A small brad secured the strips. Finished pegs were strung in dozens on a flat hazel and sold to housewives at tuppence a dozen. They lasted for twenty years or more, unless left to rot on the clothes-line.

Gipsy caravans were spotlessly clean and natty, decorated inside and out with gay ancestral patterns—much as were the barges that used to ply up and down the great Union Canal. When they were on the move most of the gipsies' bulkier domestic gear hung below the caravan, tin baths, cans, buckets, etc. A lurcher dog trotted between the back wheels. The gipsy

men were reputed to treat both their dogs and women alike:
'Beat 'em when they need it.'

The women made wonderful macramé string belts, threaded
with coloured beads in lovely patterns, craft designs reminiscent
of old Moorish tiles and Persian murals. Authority said some
were pure Burmese. With their solemn, dark-eyed babies
shawled to their hips, they came to the kitchen with baskets of
goods for sale and bundles of herbs for Cookie, collected in
meadows and hedges in their seasons. Camomile, pennyroyal,
tansy, agrimony tops and peppermint, with mousehair grass,
dug by the roots. This isn't a grass at all, but a relative of the
hawkbits, little rosettes of oval leaves, covered with tiny silvery
hairs, giving its name, mousehair. The drier the habitat the
mousier the plant. It has a bitter taste and a tiny dandelion-like
blossom. Boiled with linseed, black stick liquorice and lemons,
it was wonderful for whooping coughs, and comforting in
bronchitis of the aged. I can vouch for its efficiency in whooping
cough. Cookie was a wizard with herbs, tisanes for a variety of
inward troubles, ointments for most outside griefs and wounds.
She made cosmetics and complexion aids by the bucketful;
hair pomades for gents, hair restorer and dyes, eyebrow black,
elderflower water to cure freckles, milk of roses for 'a delicate
and undetectable bloom' on the darkest complexion, distilled
water of cucumbers 'against redness, and a saucy nose', camomile rinse, with beer, for golden hair.

There was always fun in the kitchen when the women came
with their stock-in-trade. They peddled cottons and buttons,
needles and bootlaces, ribbons and shoe-ties, lace for trousseaus.
Liz used to purchase dozens of yards of linen-thread lace for my
petticoats—torchon, childproof!

From the gipsies one could buy strings of blue beads, the
most lovely forget-me-not blue, 'for love and good luck, lovely
lady.' Who could resist the implications of that? Psychological
pedlars? They certainly knew a thing or two long before high-
pressure sales technique came on the scene. There were yellow

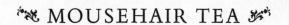 MOUSEHAIR TEA

A cure for
Whooping Cough

Into a large stewpot put:

2 gallons of Fresh Spring Water

1 quart of Linseed

4 Lemons, cut in half

1 lb of Demerara Sugar

1 lb of Stoned Raisins

2 ozs of Black Stick Liquorice

1 quart pot of Mousehair Grass Roots

AND ALL PRESSED DOWN TIGHT

Fresh Herb is preferred to the dry herb.

Boil gently and steadily until the liquid is half
consumed and the Linseed jelly-like.
Strain into a fresh pot and keep warm on the stove.

GIVE A TEACUPFUL WHEN THE
COUGHING PAROXYSMS REQUIRE.
KEEP THE CHILD'S FEET WARM.

beads, simulating amber; worn day and night they cured chest complaints or at least eased them. Perhaps belief in their efficiency was half the success? And, of course, there were the fortunes. For a sixpence they would promise the maid-servants a dark handsome husband, sometimes coming soon, sometimes from far over the sea.

For a shilling they would prophesy a quiverful of children, all as dark and handsome as their dad. Handsome or not, the lot of all married women seemed to be a quiverful, irrespective of gipsies. For bigger silver there was always a fortune and far-away travel. It was all fine and dandy, so long as Maggie or Jane didn't pay two gipsies and get contrary predictions.

The village women whispered dark tales of those cursed by gipsies for doubting their powers, of the evil eye cast on cattle. They were blamed for all misfortunes, from bed-bugs to raging toothache. Old Mrs Dence swore that her bad luck with her babies was because she had laughed at a pregnant gipsy woman who had turned and sworn at her. Quite useless to tell her that because she had given birth eight times in nine years her babies could not support the burden of life. She knew different. She clung to her curse. It set her apart.

There is no denying that the gipsies traded upon the superstitious beliefs that were current amongst country dwellers, and played upon these. Their whole way of life caused them to be mistrusted; mystery was all part of their protective colouring, to protect themselves. Treated kindly they responded likewise. I questioned Henry about spells and cursings and prophecies. He declared it was all a knack they had got. Like potting seeds in the right soil. The seed grew. They sowed the ideas and fear did the rest. If you never looked scared, nobody ever tried to scare you. Fear was the most evil force in the world. We left it like that. I went on filling thumb-pots, with nice potting soil. Henry pricked out a primula into each one. I felt comforted and secure.

One morning our doctor drove up to see Authority. He was

a worried man. There were two strange caravans on the covert clearing; Continental gipsies, not a tribe known to us at all.

The landlord of the Cricketers' had called him to see an old woman, ill in one of the caravans. He had seen her and she was dying of smallpox. She would probably pass on before sunset. He wished to remove her for isolation but the two people in the other caravan had cut up rough. They were the son and daughter-in-law of the old queen. She was the last of her tribe and must, when dead, as tribal law demanded, burn with her belongings and caravan.

It was English Civil Law versus gipsy law and protocol, a tricky situation since tribal ties were strong amongst all gipsies. Both Authority and the doctor could have wished it had happened on other territory. One could not provoke Maidstone, but to burn a dead body in the Kentish countryside? Unthinkable.

Authority said to send the Sergeant along: 'He's been vaccinated.' So Henry went. He and the gipsy's son spat on hands and clinched a deal. Henry would remove the dead body himself, and had pledged his word of honour that it should be buried without rites or a service of any kind, in an unmarked grave. The son and wife would then perform their tribal last rites, in their own way, burn the caravan and be free to depart. It was a reasonable settlement to a knotty state of affairs; most satisfactory. Once clear of the parish, pass the buck. They were not our responsibility.

Late that afternoon, armed with an old zinc bath full of discarded sheets in a strong solution of chloride of lime and carbolic, Henry and the doctor went along to the north covert. The parish bier, with a deal coffin, followed behind. The old gipsy queen was dead. Authority was already at the clearing. Bad news travels fast and there was quite a gathering of sightseers, all keeping a sanitary distance.

The coffin was placed upon the ground beside the camp-fire, P.C. Jellybelly, propped on the handlebars of his bike, watching closely. The law must be served. Henry and the doctor entered the caravan, rolled the poor corpse in the lime-soaked sheets and Henry carried it to the coffin. It was at once sealed and wheeled away. The son took a flaming branch from the fire and slung it into the interior of the caravan. His wife threw another underneath; a couple of pints of lamp-oil set things going well. A death certificate was given to the son, P.C. Jellybelly wrote in his notebook and it was over. A strange way to leave a free life and God's fresh air.

The caravan burned long into the night. By daylight the clearing was empty. Not an ash or cinder remained on the ground; all had been scattered in the wind. Where the coffin had laid was a bunch of green herbs. Civil and tribal law had been well served, peace preserved. The caravan had rested, the soul gone on its way. The gipsy queen was laid to rest before midday, close below the wall on the north side of the churchyard, where all 'died unknown, hanged, murdered or suicides' were traditionally interred—'Out of the north evil shall come.'

All the clothing Henry had worn was burned next day in smother corner, and he spent three weeks sleeping in a horse-box. Everybody on the place was vaccinated and the incident almost forgotten. Incidentally, we were not vaccinated with laboratory serum, but with lymph taken straight from a calf. The reaction was terrific, leaving scars as large as penny pieces.

CHAPTER SEVEN

Life was by no means a placid stream. Troubles came in couples and not long afterwards crisis came again, and again it was Henry who solved it.

Farmer Harvey sent to the house to say that that Tapsell, the finest thatcher in the district, had gone off his head. He had chased his wife and the baby out of their cottage in their night-clothes. Mary had taken refuge with a neighbour and he was sitting outside the only door into the neighbour's house with his thatching knives on his knees, coaxing her to bring the baby out. Luckily the windows were too small for him to try climbing in. No one could approach the cottage.

Poor Tapsell, he had always been a bit unpredictable at the

full moon, now he was over the edge. The two women were without water or milk for a cup of tea, and the tiny one was 'wailing summat pitiful.' He was inviting Mary to 'bring out babby. I'll soon quiet 'ew. Just bring it out.'

Liz and Cookie and I were helping Henry and Jack Dence to pick Ribston Pippins when the stockman from Harvey's came with the news. It was entirely Henry's pigeon. Authority was in Scotland. Even while the situation was being explained he had already decided on a plan. Going to the potting-shed he loaded the little grindstone into the wheelbarrow, together with a broken iron fence-post. He forbade anyone to go with him. In shirtsleeves and garden apron he was a well-known and trusted figure.

The cottage was a mile away. Reaching the gate Henry stopped the barrow in the lane where he had a clear view of the cottage doorway and where Tapsell could see the grindstone. Setting up the stone he began turning the handle, slowly at first with the piece of old iron on the stone. Gradually the whine of iron on stone penetrated the poor sick mind. Tapsell turned to watch Henry. He stared, while his scattered wits considered the situation.

Slowly he stood upright, fingering the edge of a knife. Henry knew he was winning. Casually, Henry called to him, 'Give it a turn on the stone, mate. You're welcome. That knife wouldn't cut butter if it was made hot. You don't want to hurt Mary.'

Tapsell came down the path to the grindstone. 'Go on,' said Henry. 'Sharpen it up a bit.' He let go the handle and Tapsell laid the knife across the stone and seized the handle. He was vulnerable. A quick rabbit punch and it was all over. From the back of an outhouse a couple of waiting county constables brought a strait-jacket, and while Henry was on his way back to pick apples, poor Tapsell was being wheeled off to hospital.

Events like these were tidal waves on our quiet shores; emotional meat and drink in humdrum, ordinary daily lives, when contact with wider horizons meant long, infrequent journeys by the carrier's cart, or long miles walking with the babies in the perambulator and those who could toddle tagging on to mammy's skirts. Not that walking was reckoned a nuisance. The countryfolk either walked or stayed put. It was nothing for quite little children to walk four or five miles to and from school, with their cold pork sandwiches in their satchels. Labourers worked from dawn to dusk on cold, boiled, pickled pork and cider, walking home at the end of the day. A good days' work was not considered the cursed necessity it has become in these softer days. It was a way of life, with a self-respecting pleasure in toil well done; pride in an honest day's work for a days' wage. It may not have been a great wage by today's reckoning. The worker may have been reckoned poor, but to be poor in the countryside was wealth compared with the sheer flea-bitten poverty in the crowded backstreets of towns.

There was always good living in the countryside. It may not have meant quantities of butcher's meat, but there was plenty besides; fresh fruit, fresh vegetables, rabbits wild and tame, pork, back-yard hens, skim-milk at a penny a quart. Eggs in times of plenty were ten for sixpence. A pint of small beer cost one penny. Cider was cheaper even than that. 'Bacca' was three-pence an ounce, and the fanciful townee cigarettes were only one penny for a packet of five. Oh, the packet of five that cured me of smoking for ever!

Friends were staying with us. They had a young hopeful of eleven years old and I looked up to him as a man of the world. He looked down on me as, pooh! only a girl. I didn't much care for his attitude. I had a penny to spend; so had he. He suggested loftily that of course at school he would have bought smokes. Smokes? Oh, yes, he had enjoyed the illicit joys of cigarettes behind the bogs. In fact he had got a couple of packets in his baggage; I could buy one if I liked, if I pinched the matches. He went for the cigarettes and I pinched the matchbox from the Bothy.

He took my penny and together we retired, secretly, to the laurels down the back drive. There, on two sacks, we sat down to a private orgy of 'bacca' smoking. We lit up like old hands and he instructed me in the art of suck in, blow out. I got on fine with the first two; he said that for a starter I was pretty good. That raised my ego. Eager to line up with his opinion I smoked two more. Suddenly I heeled sideways. I felt queasy, sick as a hound puppy. Terrible! My pal vanished, the world was spinning round me, I couldn't see. I lay on the ground, retching miserably.

Jack Dence, passing along the drive, smelt the cigarette smoke, and had to investigate, of course. Pushing through the bushes he found me, took one look and roared off to find Henry. Henry came, took one look, and rushed off to find Authority. All three came back together and had a heartless laugh at my plight. When they had laughed their fill, Henry picked me up and carried me, still retching, to the kitchen, where Cookie, more sympathetic than the menfolk, gave me a dose of ipecacuanha, whereupon I was so sick that I thought I was going to die.

Liz came and gave me a dose of castor oil and put me to bed. I slept for sixteen hours, to wake cured of smoking for all time. For weeks I was the joke of the Estate and I felt thoroughly ashamed. *Experientia docet.*

Everything that was considered 'funny ha! ha!' was good for a free half-pint on a Saturday night. An apostle from the Abode of Love came round the parish, preaching the gospel that the law which allowed a gal only one husband was just monotony. He was a pretty fast worker. He liked the lassies young and tender as French beans. He had already upset one or two young married women, and it was reputed that at least two husbands were on the warpath. The Cricketers' hummed. He was a tricky customer and husbands swore vengeance.

One day he wandered up the drive and called at the kitchen

door; his luck was out. He ran into Cookie and she pretty soon sent him to the right about, but not before he had spied the girls in the kitchen. He returned later, when the opposition had gone district-visiting with Liz. The serpent entered Eden.

He cut such a swathe with Maggie the tweeny-maid, a flighty piece if ever there was one, that she was mazed, green and silly. He started visiting her in the evenings, not in honest fashion at the back gate, but over the wall into the vegetable garden, where snug in the asparagus grass they could spoon in peace. Getting in was easy; Maggie left the laundry steps against the wall. Getting out no trouble at all. The gates were bolted inside; Maggie let him out.

Maggie was a gay, devil-may-care, little fly-by-night. She had been walking out with Billy Bennett, our carpenter, for more than a twelvemonth and Liz had promised to help her to make her wedding dress. Lately she had ducked meeting Bill; she was 'too busy,' which was a naughty fib.

Billy was normally a cheerful soul, full of jokes, sincerely and deeply attached to Maggie, jealous as Hell. He now looked like a man with murder on his mind. He took his problem to Henry in the hot-house where he was repairing the top lights. What to do? Henry was cold comfort for once. 'Nothing,' said Henry. 'One man's meat is another chap's poison,' and he reckoned Maggie was born poison. Better find it out before than after marriage. There were as good fish in the sea as ever came out of it, and if Bill felt he had to put an arm round a wench then find another.

Good advice no doubt for a flirty, kiss-and-part chap of eighteen to twenty. It wasn't like that. Poor Billy was thirty-six, Maggie his first regular, and his heart was badly cracked. He had reached the stage when he wanted the fairy off the Christmas tree and that was his Maggie.

Henry was puzzled over the state of the asparagus beds. He consulted with Jack Dence. Jack had his head screwed on the right way; a confirmed bachelor, he had suffered quite a few female cantrips in his youth and he wasn't averse to a bit of fun. He had seen the steps left out a couple of times and locked them in the stables. He would certainly keep watch and he would have a few words in the bar at the Cricketers'. A week later he reported to Henry that the disgruntled husbands were game. 'Right,' said Henry. 'We'll shift the big melon frame tomorrow; tell Billy as you go home. We shan't want the lights on it.'

The frame was moved and a large strawberry net disguised the outline. Just as dusk was closing in, the conspirators came across the big meadow, two husky farm labourers. Jack reported that the apostle of love was sneaking in the shadows along the covertside and that Maggie had just put out the steps. Billy and Jack Dence were hidden in the asparagus. Henry said he wanted no murder done and he left them to it. Billy was breathing smoke and fire.

It was just dark when the caller straddled the wall and dropped straight into the net. 'Just like a rotten plum!' said Jack next day. Maggie, all smiles, tripped down from the house just in time to see her boyfriend being rolled into a cocoon of netting by Billy and two wildly blaspheming cuckolded husbands, and to watch helplessly while they loaded him on to a handcart *en route* for Staplehurst horse-pond.

Jack took Maggie back to the kitchen, where she threw an attack of hysterics on the kitchen floor, blurting out the circumstances. Cookie came up with a dose of hartshorn and a quote. " 'Who climbeth in by any other way",' she said forbiddingly, '"that same is a thief and a robber." Here, drink this and stop that noise at once. Let that be a lesson to you, Maggie Pilcher.'

Maggie's sobs subsided. Bitterly, she sniffled, 'I'll never speak to that Bennett again. Never, never!' She was vicious.

Cookie was severe. 'Never's a long time, my girl! Bill's a good chap and you could do worse.'

Maggie was spiteful. 'A good chap? I don't want a good chap. He can't even squeeze a girl's waist all proper!'

Cook was scandalised. She stared hard at Maggie's waist-line. 'If that's only as far as he got with you, my girl, you've had a lucky escape. You . . . hussy! Squeeze a girl's waist, indeed! You get to bed.'

Maggie went. Cookie's word was law. She kept a tight hand on the girls. I'm open to bet that no cheeky fellow had ever tried to put his arm around her waist. She was pretty much the same shape up and down, nearly all waist is the best description. Of indeterminate age, so far as I could tell at an age where everybody was only a grown-up. Black hair in a great plaited bun under her cap. Eyes, dark as currants in gingerbread, looked directly at you and a world she had mastered and made her own. Honesty and kindness personified, Cookie was be-loved by all; queen of the kitchen, wedded to her profession and peerless in it. Many guests had tried to lure her from us without success.

In a house without a mistress to boss her around, she ruled supreme and supremely well. We lacked nothing she could provide for us, nor did anyone who came to us in need or trouble. She made Christmas puddings by the dozen, one for each household on the Estate and quite a few spares which Doctor Harris collected for his very poor patients. They were round puddings, boiled in linen clothes—no basins—in the big clothes coppers in the laundry. We all took a share in keeping the fire holes full of fire, for pudds that stopped boiling, if only for five minutes, went sad and cluggy. Nothing raised a better heat than ash or chestnut faggots. Hazel wasn't too bad, either; it raised a quick heat fast, but died out quickly, leaving no heat.

The boys and 'the stick insect' kept up the supply of suitable faggot wood, turn and turn with stoking. There were jobs for everybody. I always helped with raisins, big, plummy ones, and they had to be stoned. '*Only* the stones, mind, not the flesh!' Preparing the fruit was a military operation at the end of every September. Mrs Dence and Mrs Havinden came in to do the currants and sultanas. First, they were all washed—and they came in twenty-eight-pound bags, jute bags, hairy and sticky. The currants were Greek, dried on mats in the sun, filthily dirty, full of little bits of earth and stones, small black stones that were so hard to distinguish from the currants. All had to be washed under the pump until the water streamed clean, then dried on sieves. In those days there was no Whitworths behind the ready-to-use packets in a supermarket. No girl had a best friend.

Liz did the candied peel, gorgeous stuff. Halves of orange and lemon peels, each with a lovely lump of candy sugar in the hollows. Cookie did all the suet herself, to be certain that no bits of fleshy, gristly skin slipped in to vex the teeth at table. Twenty pounds of best beef-kidney suet, chopped to crumbly texture with a semi-circular steel chopper in a holly-tree bowl, dark with age and long usage.

In the laundry a great wooden bread trough was set up on trestles beside the ironing-table. Into the trough went all the ingredients as they were ready. Nutmeg, spices, almonds and sugar were added, together with a bottle of brandy and a quart of ale. All this was mixed, covered with the trough lid, and left to ripen the flavours. Next afternoon the boilers were filled and the fires lit. The ironing-table was covered with the pudding cloths ready scalded and floured. It was a time of celebration.

Cookie added the requisite quantity of flour and fine bread-crumbs and, with sleeves rolled up almost to her shoulders, plunged both hands into the mixture and pummelled away until she was satisfied that it was mixed. This was the great moment. All in the house gathered for the ceremonial adding of the luck. Authority was first; into the mixture he emptied a bank bag of threepenny bits and took a stir. One after the other we all followed. It was such fun.

Most of us lingered until Cookie had given the whole mass a distributing turnover, doled out the mixture into the cloths and the first batch of pudds was merrily boiling. Henry and Jack sat up long after the rest of us were in bed. Those pudds had to boil for eight hours. When done they were lifted out on to sieves and when they were cold each was brushed with brandy and a new cloth covering added. They kept wonderfully.

The stirring ceremony seemed to me, even when I was very small, to be something very special, something that preserved a bond between us all. Perhaps it was all bound up with the few words of Hindustani which Authority muttered as he spilled the threepenny bits all over the pudding mixture. The bits were of silver in those days, and we were not germ-conscious as we have since become. Anyway, they were well boiled. I never heard either that anybody got choked or broke a tooth on one. We were all too busy examining our helping for the bit of luck that would last throughout the year ahead. When I look back to those times, I now wonder so often what, oh, what would be Cookie's reaction to the suggestion of a Christmas pudding bought ready-made in the supermarket?

Authority's Christmas box went to each home along with the pudding. A hamper filled, according to the number in the family, with a piece of beef, a cock pheasant, and a bottle of port, with a cake and two hundredweight of best coals. To this Cookie added a pound of tea, nuts and oranges and a box of crackers. Logs were free for the cutting in the coppices.

All this was not a charitable handout, nor was it received as such. It was a Christmas gift in goodwill to all. Throughout the length and breadth of England the old landed families did the same. The commercially wealthy had still to learn the way around; they had come up late.

The oranges came by the crate, ten shillings for three hundred fruits, each wrapped in tissue-paper. They came from Spain mostly and could be bought retail at forty-eight for a shilling. Coals came by the truck load, straight from the colliery, six pounds sterling per ten-ton load, free on rail to the nearest goods depot, in our case Ashford Junction. It arrived after harvest, when carts and labourers were free to haul it, and all the menfolk looked forward to the arrival. It was a change of routine, with free beer and a good lunch provided. It was also a throat-drying job.

I went once with Henry to see the trucks unloaded—only once. When we got back Liz took one look at me. 'My gracious! Oh, you dirty little pickle! No more of that for you, my lady! Where's Henry's sense? It'll take a week of boiling to get those petticoats white!' and she went for Henry. 'Bald-headed,' he said, which meant no holds barred.

It was like water off a duck's back, she complained. Just like talking to oneself. Poor Liz; if I didn't look like something out of a cardboard box she took it as a personal insult to herself.

In the country one bought in quantity: we used to buy our flower pots in bulk also, from Messrs Sankey's Kilns, a whole kiln of pots, free on rail for thirty shillings. Over two hundred pots in assorted sizes, from big twelve-inch chrysanthemum pots, down through the range to the tiddly little thumb-pots for seedlings, all packed as carefully as table china, in straw-filled packing cases. Solid, non-returnable cases that came in so useful when empty. Henry built me a hen-house out of two cases for my bantams. Godfather gave me a bantam family for a birthday present when I was six, six dainty, biscuit-coloured little ladies and a cockbird, all game-bred aristocrats. That tiny cockbird—he weighed less than two pounds—remains one of the loveliest things I have ever seen, scarlet and gold and metallic green, with a noble tail of arching green feathers, exquisite little spurred feet lifting off the ground as though it was only just good enough to walk upon.

'Proud as Lucifer,' said Authority, and we called him Lucifer. He was a little feathered devil. He hated competition, and squared up to any cock pheasant in the coverts who even looked a come-hither at his harem. Havinden said he had mangled quite a few, and that he had guts and no weight.

To thrive, bantams must have free range. They are insect-eaters and hen-run conditions do not really suit them; they always came home to roost. Proud was Lucifer and pride his fall. Along one side of the orchard Cookie had installed a hen-house and run, with a number of Plymouth Rock fowls. The Plymouth Rock cockbird was a giant. Beside him Lucifer was a mere wisp, yet he hated that Rock on sight. It was a declaration of war. He cursed hate and vulgarities at the big bird through the wire netting; he forgot his little ladies, to spend hours strutting up and down outside the run growing thin with hate. The big cockerel, in security, didn't give a damn. He stood high on his toes, flapping his wings, stretching his ugly, scaly legs to yell 'cock-a-doodle-do' in a really triumphant challenge.

It had to come to battle some time, and for the bantam it couldn't be too soon. It was Cookie with the egg basket who provided the chance. She opened the door into the roost and never noticed, as she rifled the nest-boxes, that the imp had nipped in behind her, out through the hen-hole and into the run. Nobody saw the preliminary square-up. The battle must have raged all the morning, until the big fellow was dead, and Lucifer lay dying beside him. There was blood everywhere. Henry held me close whilst I wept buckets, before we buried them both together in the nut-walk. Henry said that was proper, because he was sure they had gone where all good fighters go. I had finished with keeping bantams. Havinden took the six little ladies to foster pheasant eggs and they made wonderful little mothers.

It was Cookie's hen-run that late one summer gave me the fright of my life. A fright, which to recall, can still make me creepy. It had been a bad summer, wet and damp, when soft fruits had musted before they were ripe and the jargonelle pears on the stable walls had developed rotten brown 'wasp' spots before they were eatable, when tipsy bluebottle flies and a few Red Admiral butterflies clung to, and spoilt, all the wild blackberries along the hedges. It was, said Havinden, whose baby pheasants had been decimated by cold and damp, a famine year.

Pottering round on an after-breakfast nosey tour, I approached the hen-run. The hens were all huddled together in a corner, uttering short startled clucks. Suddenly, their fear was mine. The early air was warmish, dank and sweaty, and the whole floor of the run was split across from corner to corner, heaving at an angle of forty-five degrees. It seemed to be moving. I felt my scalp tighten, even as I stared cold shivers ran down my spine and my legs wilted. It was real blue funk. My throat was dry. The crack was packed with a solid mass of white knobs like eggs and, as the watery sun got a little stronger, the gap was widening. Those things were after me. Run! Run! My feet wouldn't move. I fell on the path screaming in panic.

Jack Dence, who was hunting for filberts and cobs in the nut walk, came tearing along. Terrified, I could only point to the horror, and the poor scared hens. Back in the house I was comforted by Cookie, whilst Jack, with Henry and Authority, went to investigate. They reported mushrooms, a great mass of them below the floor of the run; the surface crust, packed solid by droppings and the feet of three dozen hens, was rising like the lid of a basket. Thousands and thousands of mushrooms. Nothing to be scared of, come and see.

I went, reluctantly, with Liz and Cookie. It was a most unlovely sight. After several days a farm wagon brought a load of hot lime from the Cranbrook gas-works, Bennett and Henry shifted the run and burned the hen-house and the obscenity was scotched.

The real responsibility for the upheaval was Henry's. A couple of years before he had used an old out-house, fully two hundred yards away, to start a mushroom-bed, but the temperature was not steady enough and not so much as a button had come up. The mycelium had spread underground and eventually 'smelt' the hen-run. August had been a month of moist, humid, sweaty weather. 'Plum fever weather,' said old Mrs Dence, 'when milk turns sour before it leaves the cow and kids get bowel rumbles and painful innards.' That was August, and the atmosphere just right for the phenomenon we had experienced.

I was only a little girl. Mushrooms, magical in green meadows under a moonlit sky, under a pink dawn sky, at sun-up, white as milk and perfect; those I knew and loved. But a solid phalanx, menacing, primitive power on the march? A thousand times no! What I knew and understood I never feared. Authority borrowed a book from the vicarage and spent a whole afternoon reading to me, all about toadstools and mushrooms, mycelium and the like. Much of it was way beyond my comprehension, but I took in the gist.

CHAPTER EIGHT

In Kent that autumn almost every hop-grower lost his labour and his cash. Disease ravaged the hop gardens. The bines hung black and rotting. The smell was awful.

At Harvey's they grew a rather special sort of hop. Sturdier in the vine, the bunches bore bigger hops in compact clusters, like muscat grapes. When the shoots were being thinned in spring Henry would go to the gardens and get a basketful for Cookie. Boiled like asparagus with plenty of melted butter they were a delicious vegetable. The pickers were keen on this variety of hop. It picked quickly and easily, with no bits of leaf to spoil a well-picked bin when the tallyman came round with the bushel basket.

When the vines were growing well up the strings it was pleasant to walk through the alleys between rows with Liz and Henry. One unforgettable Sunday afternoon I caught a hop-dog, not a four-legged beastie but a caterpillar, magnificent to see, three inches long, clothed in rich, creamy, yellow fur, his sides stashed with velvety-black, and at his tail end a half-inch tuft of pinkiest mauve hairs. A hop-dog was every country child's dream, so rarely seen as to be almost legendary. I have never seen another one. I coaxed him into my sun-bonnet and carried him back to my bedroom where he joined my menagerie.

I had a wild bees' nest slung in a net from the curtain pole and they came and went as they liked through the open sash; little, silvery-yellow bees they were, like tiny bumble-bees. Henry had found the nest when clearing a bank beside the lake. I also had a formicarium with a sliding glass panel through which the ants might be watched at work. The Vicar gave me that. I had a dormouse, fat and lazy, in a cage. He was a joy to me; sitting on his haunches he would hold a cherry in his little front paws and peel it delicately with his teeth before eating the flesh off the stone. Henry shocked me by telling me that the Romans had considered dormice as great delicacies and actually fattened them for table, calling them *glis glis* because they were so delicious. I tore the picture of Julius Caesar out of my history book. And on a visit to London Henry had bought me a lovely green lizard in a glass tank. He ate meal-worms from Harvey's pig meal. All these creatures were of endless interest to me; and now they were eclipsed by the rare beauty of the hop-dog.

The Curate, Mr Mulholland, told me that it would become a most beautiful moth if I fed it regularly on hop leaves. One day Henry came along with a bundle of wheat straws cut short. He said he thought the hop-dog was ready to cocoon; it had stopped eating and looked torpid. Henry was right; in a few days the hop-dog had spun itself a most beautiful cradle trimmed with all his yellow fur. We put the box with the cocoon into the cold green-house because Henry said the moist atmosphere would help to split the case at the right time. Everybody seemed keen to see the moth, when this happened. We watched it every day for what seemed to me weeks and weeks but we never saw the moth. It hatched in the night and sailed off through the ventilator. It was a bitter disappointment. All I had left was a bunch of straw and the little empty cradle; such a beautiful thing, a marvel that no ingenuity of man could match.

Hop-picking time was fun. We didn't grow any on the place, but, as was to be expected in hop-growing country, the hedges were all full of strays. Liz and I would pick these for stuffing 'sleepy pillows' and Cookie would bargain with the tallyman for a couple of 'pooks' before they all went to the oasts.

Hops for sleepy pillows must not be kiln-dried, but done naturally, spread out in an airy place. We made no end of sleepy pillows; every one of our beds had one, a large linen bag filled with a proper quantity each of hops and dried cowslips, dried in their season. Authority always carried one in his kit, our guests begged to be allowed to keep one. Godfather said that after a day in Whitehall he was thankful to get his head on one. I learnt to sew, making those linen bags, seaming and felling. 'A very proper exercise for all ladies, teaching them to have a care for others.'

I was handier with a trowel than with needle and thread. I stitched my forefinger to the linen so often that it was sore, and a proper exercise became dire penance. But there was no reneging under Liz's eye. I stitched and bled when I would far rather have been out with Henry sowing seeds.

It was always good to watch Henry sowing seeds, rubbing them out gently and evenly between finger and thumb. Small dusty seeds like primulas were first mixed with a little silver sand, being sown on the surface of the boxes and firmed to the soil with a patter, just a block of wood with a handle of nails.

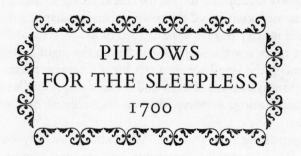

PILLOWS
FOR THE SLEEPLESS
1700

Of strong linen, close woven. A strip fifteen inches wide and thirty-six deep. Fold to make a bag, eighteen inches deep. Seam and fell all sides, leaving a space one end to admit the stuffing.

Take of cowslips and fresh hops, newly dried, as many as you deem enough to make a soft stuffed cushion in equal parts. Distribute your hops and cowslips nicely, in a bowl, and proceed to stuff your pillow until you feel it comfortable to the head. Over-sew the opening and your pillow is made.

Those who by reason of great grief, study or long watchfulness cannot catch their sleep will find such a pillow serviceable.

On seed-sowing he had a lot of pithy maxims. 'Sow thin and reap mean,' he'd often tell the boys. Sometimes it was, 'Too thin, sow again,' depending on the type of seed, and with really plentiful seed he would advise, 'Sow thick and thin well.' It used to be said that parsley seed went to the devil for seven weeks before sprouting. Ours didn't. Some parsley plants were always left to run to seed. These were cut when ready, tied in bunches and hung on the wall of the vegetable garden. They sprouted almost as soon as the seed dropped on the soil and were then transplanted into rows. No devilling in our garden.

Henry never had a bed of carrots, only single rows between rows of peas and broad beans, and carrot seed was never sown without a tablespoonful of ground cayenne pepper and a pinch of lettuce seed, the pepper to chase it up and the lettuce to mark the rows and make hoeing easier, and all the precautions were to fox carrot-flies. Henry said the fly was a bad dodger, that it liked a clear run over which to drop its eggs and that the pea and bean rows took its mind off the carrots. It's certain that we never had maggoty carrots.

One hears a great deal of grumbling amongst gardeners today that seed is germinating badly. It's also certain that gardeners are getting more impatient to see results and seed is being sown into the earth before the temperature will nurture it. It rots before it can sprout. Sow in March, says the seed packet. But March can be as cold as the Arctic Circle, the chills of February lingering deep in the soil, even though the wind is blowing and the sun trying to shine. Wait until the sun has power to heat up the poker. That's not as daft as it sounds. All our ground for seeding was well prepared and then left to warm up. The time for sowing was determined by an old steel poker thrust nine inches deep into the soil. Each midday Henry would withdraw it, hold it against his face just like Liz testing a smoothing-iron. When the poker was warm enough, time was right. The surface was raked over and seeding down began.

Henry liked to see plenty of treading space between rows.

His words were always the same. 'Wider, boy! Wider! You've got plenty of room. If your boots are tens, not less than fifteen inches between rows. Space out, boy! Space out! You want room to move. Your seeds want room to grow. Our garden isn't a back-yard.'

I often marvel at the array of chemical aids now considered necessary by the modern gardener. All short cuts no doubt, but when did short cuts produce anything worth achieving? What residual after-effects do all these aids leave behind? Have chemists and scientists forgotten the basic truth that nothing on earth is an end product of itself? That all chemicals used to destroy this and that may, after long and continual use, so pile up and combine within the soil that they may end by actually poisoning the crops they are meant to protect? They may even destroy the fertility of earth herself, to say nothing of human existence. Old-time gardeners faced exactly the same earth and insect problems as the men of today, yet they did as well, or even better, and what they produced had taste and quality. The hoe was the best weed-killer of all; it left the dying weeds to nourish the soil. A bucket of weed-killer may be cheaper and quicker but you're poorer in the end.

All old gardeners had their favourite sprays against insects. Soft soap, boiled with quassia chips in rainwater and laced with paraffin, was a favourite for greenfly on roses. It wasn't a once-and-for-all remedy; it had to be repeated once a week, apparently because greenfly don't lay eggs, they lay insects. You can kill the parent greenfly, but the nippers will still hatch strong and lively. For blackfly on broad beans, Henry used an old household remedy guaranteed to kill fleas, bugs, moths and beetles. It was sovereign and non-poisonous to human beings. For caterpillars on cabbages he swore by lukewarm salt and water; even cuckoo-spit on the lavender hedge succumbed to that. Our very special recipe for spray was a mixture of pyrethrum, which we grew, soft soap, shag 'bacca' and fully grown rhubarb leaves, all boiled down with rainwater to a thick treacly liquid, strained through muslin into a tub, and kept ready for diluting. Half a pint of 'stinker' to two gallons of water. It was a killer once and for all. Soft soap came in twenty-gallon barrels, funny, thick stuff, like greeny-brown jelly, much liked by mothers for washing hair on Saturday nights. Rats loved the spillage down the side of the barrel.

One morning I heard all hell coming from the store-shed. Looking in I saw the lid on the soap barrel was askew and the row was coming from inside the barrel. I lifted the lid and down in the soft soap were three large brown rats, trapped up to their bellies in the soap. When they saw me they bared their teeth and tried to jump at me. I dropped the lid and went for Henry to come and see what we had caught. There was nothing to do but push them well down under the surface and leave them to their fate. The 'stick insect' buried them in the dung-hill and Henry forbade me ever again to try and get close to a rat. He said that when they were trapped they were as dangerous as tigers, and as cunning as the very devil. He also declared that owing to the panic screaming of the trapped rats no rats would come near the store for months; the screams had warned the rest of danger. Remarkable to say, they didn't.

Havinden, the keeper, was most plagued by rats. They stole his pheasants' eggs and ate the baby birds. He had a story which illustrated what Henry had said about rats being cunning. He set a large wire box-trap in the hatchery and caught an old doe rat expecting a litter. Understandably she screeched. Havinden picked up the trap on the prongs of a pitchfork and dropped the lot into a water butt, drowning her. He then reset the trap. Rats and fleas are never lonely and he had seen several around, but still the trap remained unsprung. He remarked it in the bar of the Cricketers' Arms one night and a gipsy boy, drinking and listening, spoke up. He said that the frightened rat had left the scent of fear on the trap and Havinden had left his own scent on the wires, so no rat would enter the trap.

He advised that when setting the trap Havinden should handle a piece of bloater or kipper bones before baiting the hook, preferably with a strong bait. Havinden laughed. He had been a game-keeper for years and he had never heard such nonsense. It was just gipsy gas.

The next day he put another crust in the trap and went on hoping. Not long afterwards he was filling the incubator lamps when a rat came into the hatchery. He watched it. It didn't seem at all frightened. It walked round the trap, sniffing it delicately, examined the door, then entered the trap and looked at the hook and the mechanism, but made no move to take the crust. Then it went away, to return in a few minutes with another rat. The two of them repeated the inspection and sat to consider the situation. Then the second, longer rat, began to push the trap across the floor. Together they pushed it to the wall before capsizing it on to its side. The trap was sprung by the impact and the bait lay on the wires. The two rats ate what they could pull through until the bait was all gone.

The whole process was repeated two or three times, though Havinden only saw the first time. Then he remembered what the gipsy boy had said, so he asked Cookie for a bloater, and again set the trap, using the head of the bloater as bait. It hadn't been in place more than an hour before it was sprung and two rats were in the cage. Greed had beaten cunning. Although Havinden had no use for the gipsies, he allowed they knew a thing or two. Henry said Havinden was learning fast.

The Havindens lived in the lodge at the front gates. I liked Mrs Havinden although I considered she was a little too prim. She had been a smart ladies' maid when she met Havinden, one of the household upper crust. She had never forgotten this and was always telling the maids how she had to sit up until the small hours of the morning waiting to cut her ladyship out of her ball dresses. It seemed that Sally had to sew her into her dresses each time she dressed her; her figure was so lovely, there was no room for the bulk of buttons and hooks and eyes. Said Sally Havinden with pride, 'I made all her dresses and fitted her so that she always looked as if she'd been poured into them!'

She evidently couldn't do much for Havinden. He always looked as if he had been dressed with a hay-rake, even on Sundays, but he was such a nice kind man—except to gipsies and poachers. Then he was on the war-path. He was tall and thin, with a stern face that wrinkled into the nicest smile when he met you along the covertsides. He and Henry got along famously, although Havinden had long forgotten the number of times he'd taken Henry's wet boots off. They worked hand in glove.

CHAPTER NINE

Although Henry had a vocabulary that could take on a barrack-room flavour, he used only one naughty word in everyday commerce. Watching the awkward squad bedding out small plants, he would explode, 'Oh, hold the poor, bloody thing straight!' It was, I suppose, inevitable that I should pick up this word, though as much as my life was worth to say it. It would have meant no butter on my bread for a fortnight. Henry, too, would have scarified me. Authority used to roll out, 'Damn and set fire to it.' But he never had to do without butter; come to that, neither did Henry. I promised myself that when I grew up I would have a good cuss-up every day. It was funny, but when I grew up it didn't seem to matter any longer.

Time rolled on. Our beloved old Queen was dead. A new monarch on the throne and the Boer was settled. Peace brooded over us and national pride was high. Someone suggested that we plant a tree, a victory oak, to live for a thousand years. It was a grossly sentimental period. The idea was appealing. The local influentials, with the Vicar and churchwardens, went into a huddle. Plant a tree? Yes. Where? It was not just any tree. It must be planted in thanksgiving as well as commemoration. It must be inside the churchyard wall. There was a suitable spot. Carried unanimously.

The next question was who should plant it. It was, after all, a great occasion. The Vicar had once met a very minor foreign royalty at a continental spa, and they had corresponded. The invitation was sent, there was a gracious acceptance and the date was fixed. Authority asked Henry to choose and pot up a nice sapling before the sap began to rise. Preparations were worked out carefully. The district buzzed.

We had the firm promise of a detachment of Volunteers and the band from HQ Canterbury. As the date got nearer, willing hands set to work erecting a stage and covered stand. Henry dug and prepared the planting site. Standing spaces were roped off for the soldiers and the band, all ropes pipe-clayed white as a bandmaster's gloves. Spaces were made for the school children and an enclosure for grown-ups. The choir and portable harmonium were positioned just inside the churchyard wall.

The vestry was raided for spare cushions to make the ladies comfortable on the stand. Yards and yards of bunting, with strings of flags, were dressed overall. We did it well.

The great day dawned hot and sunny, the sky a brassy blue bowl. 'King's weather!' was everybody's salutation. Jack Dence drove the wagonette to the scene in the early morning and decorated the front of the stage with an edging of blue lobelias, with great chysanthemum pots at the corners full of scarlet Paul Cranpels and white marguerites, specially grown for the occasion. It was a day for white frocks and socks and black patent strap shoes; the hotter it got the tighter they were. By midday folks were arriving from miles around, the womenfolk to sit gossiping on the churchyard wall, the men making a bee-line for a free pint at the inn. The Volunteers spilled heartily out of their breaks, red-faced and sweating in their heavy uniforms; they also went for a free pint. School children, gathered, shining with soap and water, resplendent in their red, white and blue sashes, their patriotic hair-ties holding bunches of rag curls that would be pumpwater-straight before night. Each boy sported on his jacket a red, white and blue rosette as big as a tea saucer, with a penny-sized portrait of the King in the centre.

Liz allowed me only a discreet shoulder-knot of ribbon, but Authority gave me a little gold pin with the Royal Cypher to wear—I still have it. I have, also, the more feminine one that he gave me for the Diamond Jubilee of Queen Victoria.

The school children were fizzing with excitement at the thought of joys to come later—tea and cakes, three-legged races, sack races, army tugs-of-war, egg-and-spoon races and, when night had fallen, fireworks, great set pieces by Pain's Fireworks, and masses of crackers and rockets *ad lib*. Spirits were high. I fizzed as well; I had a passion for fireworks. Some of the boys got cocky, a couple of braggarts started a shindy but a sharp clip on the ear from the Curate soon put a damper on them.

The church clock struck two. The choir filed from the vestry to stand in a semi-circle behind the harmonium. Their well-starched white surplices stood out like angel's wings on the scallywags of the Sunday school. The organist and the Vicar were chatting in the gateway. Society was arriving. The carriages were depositing loads of chiffon flounces and lacy parasols, a flower garden of dames. The Curate escorted them to the stand, watched eagerly and critically by little girls and their mothers. Many a determination to possess frippery was born that day as they whispered among themselves.

A frosty silence suddenly descended. The Vicar's wife in

mauve mousseline rustled across the churchyard looking more like Cookie's egg-timer than ever. She eyed us all sharply as she passed in front of us on her way to her seat at the end of the row. She gave me a sideways look and I cuddled next to God-father. Liz gave me a sly nip. I stared at Mrs Vicar and thought how much nicer Liz looked in her pink poplin, even Cookie in her silver-grey alpaca was more suitably dressed.

I stared up at the Union Jack floating gently above the church tower, and at the dozens of little flags decorating the trees. All present and correct. I was certain that Authority there on the platform, in full uniform with all his ribbons up, was the finest person there, excepting of course Henry at the side guarding the little tree and the ceremonial spade. Old England was at her traditional best. Peace descended. We were ready and waiting. Somebody bumped the big drum by mistake. Some-body shushed angrily. The church clock struck three. Royalty was late!

'Hush!' whispered Liz. 'That's royalty's privilege.' Weeks later, when she told me that punctuality was the politeness of princes, I could only conclude that politeness was a movable feast. The sun beamed on us. The waiting children began shifting from one hot foot to the other. It was after the quarter-past. Godfather whispered that the Mess had sat late over lunch. I fidgeted and heaved a gusty sigh. Liz gave me another sly nip behind. Suddenly, there it was, a sibilance, like the passage of wind across an oatfield. Hats off! Royalty was at the gate. A sharp command and the military came to the present. The bandmaster raised his baton. The drums rolled, a long spine-thrilling shiver, and crashing out it came, *God Save Our Gracious King*! Full-throated it came, barriers down. Full-hearted, all sang, some through tears for those who would never return. It is ever so. To the last line we sang, while our guest stood in the gateway beside the Vicar.

He was a curious little man, short and fat. He looked just like a tubby little piglet in a grey lounge suit and a curly King

Edward trilby, the only person present who sported no ribbon. The last strains of the anthem died away. The minor royalty was warmly welcomed and replied as warmly. Backs were scratched all round. The Vicar said the Lord's Prayer and his little patriotic piece. The committee said theirs. Authority stood up, spoke up, and shut up. It was the guest's turn. He was honoured, etc., etc. Amidst a gale of handclaps, he was helped off the platform and escorted to the hole.

Henry advanced with the sapling, saluted and knelt to cut the wet sacking from the roots and spread them on the prepared soil. A stake with a label was already in place. Henry tested the stake, rose to his feet, handed over the ceremonial spade, stepped back three paces, saluted crisply and stood away, leaving the minor royalty to the job.

I had a sudden conviction that our guest had never, never handled a spade in his life before. He was holding it like a pudding-spoon. I agonised. Oh, the poor tree! I had an urge to go and help; it would die. The sapling took a list to port and from somewhere a small voice piped up, 'Oh, hold the poor bloody thing straight!' Mine? To this day I don't know how it got out; I was only thinking it to myself. From among the bandsmen there came a sudden yelp of laughter, suddenly silenced. I knew a hot wave of shame. From the seated company on the stand behind us came a long shocked hiss, like a kettle boiling over on a hot stove. There was a taste of white cotton gloves bleached in chloride of lime in my mouth as Liz clapped a hand over it. Godfather's hand came down on my shoulder, reassuring, controlling. I wanted to bolt for cover and he knew it. All eyes were on me.

I looked at Authority's back, stiff as a ramrod. He was angry; I knew the signs. Henry was again on his knees, scrabbling the earth amongst the roots. Our guest was bending low over the spade, his shoulders shaking; the ceremony was continuing. I shivered uncontrollably, hot and cold by turns, feeling the Vicar's wife staring daggers at poor Liz. Oh, how diminished

I felt. I don't recall how the next half-hour slipped by. As the last strains of the Old Hundredth died away I was withdrawn from decent society. Cookie left to go and help with the tea on the glebe; Godfather, Liz and I waited at the gate for our carriage. The Vicar's wife swept up to us and I got behind Liz. The crowd around were all ears. 'A terrible example to the school children,' she said acidly. 'A most shocking exhibition! It's time that child was sent away to school to be properly brought up.' She made Liz look small in front of all the company; that was an ill-bred thing to do. I felt I hated her. I believe I did. How could she be so rude? She moved off and I made my very ugliest face at her back.

Liz didn't answer, nor did she curtsey. The carriage came up, and Godfather lifted me in and sat beside me with his arm comforting me. As we bowled along through our lovely Kentish lanes, where tangles of dog-roses and elderflower moons bent low over banks with mauve scabious and lacy cow parsley, I wept bitterly for Liz. I had not wanted to be naughty, or wished her to be hurt; I would have died first. Godfather wiped my face, and made me blow my nose on his handkerchief, bidding me not to cry. There were, he said, times and places for all things. I had just misjudged the time, so cheer up and remember, all your life, stand by whatever you say, never run from anything. Face up to all, it's easier.

Home at last. I was escorted straight upstairs to my bedroom, to purge my debt to society. While I undressed myself and tidied away my clothes, Liz cleaned away all possibility of amusement. I was skint; all toys, all books, my dollies, my paint-box, the lot, nothing left, not even my dormouse. Solitary confinement on bread and water for twenty-four hours. No matches, no candlestick, no dessert downstairs with Authority and Godfather, no goodnight kisses, nothing! I was in choky. There were no comforting sounds at all, only the sparrows, when it got dusk, coming home to roost in the ivy outside my window; and when they had settled their roosting squabbles there would be silence in which to meditate on my sins. As dusk came down a shift of wind brought faraway whispers of band music, not tunes, only tantalising reminders of the fes/ tivities, gall and wormwood.

My mind was troubled. Why, why, why, if grown/ups could cuss freely, why was I in bed? I resolved that I would have that out with Henry. After dark, the small slice of sky that I could see through my window was speckled with tiny points of scarlet and green where the festive rockets were bursting. So was my heart. I turned on to my face and cried myself to sleep.

Next morning the Vicar's wife came round after Authority before ten/thirty. She gave him a rough time; she complained that Liz had not answered when spoken to, had not curtseyed to her and, in short, had not shown the proper respect an under should show one of the uppers. That angered Authority, for Liz was not an under. Hers was a responsible position, which she was filling well. The Vicar's wife also said that, whether he was aware of it or not, in her opinion it was time I was sent away to school. She rattled on but he wasn't to be stampeded by anyone. He regretted my lapse, no one more, but loyalty within the coop was a tradition in the army. He understood my lapse; years after he admitted it was really damn funny and years after I saw that it must have been. One of the most splendid things about him was his gift of sympathetic comprehension. He was satisfied with the way I was shaping under Liz and Henry; when ready, I would go away to school, not before. This he told her firmly before, forgetting her T.T. activities, he offered her a glass of Madeira and some cake. She refused the offer frostily and swept out. 'Good morning!'

Leaning from my window, I could see her pony/chaise on the gravel below. It struck me that if I could scare the pony and get it moving there might be some fun. I could throw something down, but what? My snowstorm paperweight would be just the thing. I was a bit late letting go and it hit the gravel just behind her as she left the front doorway. Authority opened the chaise door for her and she was gone. He picked up the paper-weight and carried it indoors. I felt just awful inside. A little while later Cookie came up to see me. She brought my snow-storm and put it down without comment. She gave me a dozen sticky cake cherries in a bit of paper and said that Liz wanted me to dress and take a walk with Authority.

I knew the joy of absolution. In the last half hour I had come to know myself. I was a real bad Blister. I might have killed the Vicar's wife with the paperweight but then she had tried to diminish Liz, my Liz, with the sweet face and plaited coronet of soft brown hair, who had looked so elegant in her pink poplin dress. All this I explained to Authority, as we walked the covertside. He didn't say much. We passed the keeper's larder and I wished that Mrs Vicar was hanging along-side the rest. My penitence was not of a lasting nature.

A few weeks later Authority told me I had been entered for school in the autumn, at a select and most selective academy for the daughters of army, navy and professional gentlemen on the other side of the county. But fate took a hand, and it was to be another year before I could go.

I broke a leg and lay for four long months flat on my back. To Henry's skilled first aid and loving care of me I owe the fact that I still have that leg. I deserved all I had to suffer, for 'deliberate and wicked disobedience'. It was all because of my efforts at impressing a rather cocky male of the species, Cyril—brother of my smoking effort—a year or so older than myself, lofty on the heights of the fourth form at Wellington, all spit and blow, despising girls. He started bragging. So did I. I didn't dare—Oh, yes I did—Back and forth it went until I got ratty. I'd show him! I burgled the implement store at Harvey's, pushed him in through the window and climbed in after him—there! But I hadn't foreseen that he would fiddle with the machinery. A large iron wheel fell on me and, doubled up, I was pinned to the floor. I felt my leg snap and screamed in agony. Cyril was no Galahad. He had no guts, said Henry afterwards. He stared at what he had done and was out of the window like lightning; screaming with sheer terror, he dashed across the countryside. I struggled for a bit and lay still, then started to struggle again. The wheel wouldn't move.

Authority, out riding, at peace with the world, left the coverts just as the frightened warrior burst screaming through the hedge. Recognising panic, he caught him, shook him into coherence and got the story. Inside minutes everybody had their orders and Authority rode off to find the doctor, the boy to pack his bag. Henry and Havinden were to come to me, Jack Dence to the stables for a handcart, and to the kitchen for blankets and hot bottles. Henry later told me that when he and Havinden got to me I was unconscious from loss of blood. They straightened me out after lifting the wheel, which weighed a hundredweight. With Havinden's cravat and a piece of wood Henry applied a tourniquet to my thigh. The high boots so fashionable today are no new thing; they were equally fashionable seventy years ago, glove-soft and lacing from insteps to knees. It was my good fortune that I was wearing a pair. Havinden went back out of the window and Farmer Harvey came and unlocked the doors. I remember blinking in the sudden flood of light.

Jack Dence and one of the lads arrived with Liz's ironing-board and a couple of stone hot-water bottles and rugs in the handcart. Strapped to the board I was laid in a bed of hay on the cart, covered closely and wheeled, not the secret way I'd come across country but down the lane to the highway and so home, and laid on the dining-room table to await the doctor. I must have stayed conscious to some extent, for I can recall staring up at the big lamp above the table and starting to whimper. Henry reminded me that wounded soldiers never cried and I dried up. Cookie brought me a large mug full of hot sugar-and-water, and Liz wept for the two of us. Henry got busy cutting a pair of splints and padding them whilst we waited for Authority and

Doctor Harris. It seemed an age and Liz said I slept. I came to with Authority holding my hands firmly in his, while the doctor cut my smart boot off in strips with my stocking.

The damage was horrible. A compound fracture with a couple of inches of shinbone through the skin. I heard Authority say, 'Can you save it?' and the doctor say he had seen worse. He probably had; he had doctored on a fast clipper for a few trips when he had first qualified. Authority took a firmer grip on my hands. Henry held my head and shoulders whilst the fracture was reduced and the splints applied.

'Ah! Lovely green bones!' said the doctor, and asked Cookie for a large broad-bladed cooking knife and a jug of boiling water. I caught what he said! Green bones? Big knife? Boiling water? I wasn't standing for butchery. I tried to struggle. 'Henry!' Willing hands kept me still while Henry said that my bones were still 'green' because I was only a little tree, not yet hard-wooded. Boiling water was to soften the roll of surgical plaster, the knife to roll it on the splint, that was all. That quietened me. Henry had said so.

Jack Dence and Havinden carried my bed down to the room Authority used for his office. It had a door on to the garden; I wouldn't be isolated. Authority moved into the bookroom opposite, across the hall. They carried me to bed, still on the ironing-board, and eased me off on to the flat mattress; there, pinioned in sandbags and with a wooden cradle to hold the bed clothes off my legs, I sweated it out, three weeks of excruciating purgatorial pain, always worse at night. For a week I grizzled and moaned. My toes jerked and pained most cruelly. I was as sick as a dog. No peace at all, no let-up. Neither Authority nor Doctor held with drops of laudanum for children. It wouldn't last long, everything seemed to be going well. The first days went by and Liz was worn out. Godfather sent two trained nurses from St Thomas's Hospital; that cut Liz to the heart. Love is so easily bruised. Cookie, quick to sense this, said she would do a turn. She wanted no starched-up madams invading her kitchen, too fussy they were by half, they wanted a maid. That didn't please Henry. Her job was to see to jellies and beef tea and feed us all; everybody had to keep their strength up. *He* was going to do night duty. Liz could have a truckle bed next to mine, he was having an arm-chair at the foot of my bed.

'Settle it amongst yourselves,' said Authority, and went off with my Godfather for a week in London, before seeing him off to America. Night after night for three more weeks, Henry sat in the chair, one hand under the cradle holding my toes so that they couldn't twitch; they still hurt but not so badly. I was comforted and, bit by bit, I slept. Jack and the lads did Henry's outside work and he slept by day. Authority was delighted. Soon I was sleeping all night.

The recuperative powers of childhood are marvellous. I knew boredom and claimed more and more of Henry's daylight hours. He must read to me. Somehow, whilst he was there I felt safe. My favourite book was *The Ingoldsby Legends*. The rhythm fascinated me; I could listen for hours and see everything happening, the Kentish background, *Smuggler's Leap*, *Grey Dolphin*, *The Jackdaw of Rheims*, *Jerry Jarvis's Wig*, *The Milkmaid's Story*, over and over again. For years I could quote yards of the *Smuggler's*. Then one day came the wonder gift.

The *crêpe* paper craze was sweeping New York and, on his return, Godfather brought me a cutting outfit, with patterns and a veritable rainbow of coloured paper. It opened a new world for me. I could manipulate paper and wires whilst still flat on my back. Creative instinct was born. Henry cut out petals and leaves for me, faithful to nature, and I made up the flowers so that they looked almost real. We showered everybody with bouquets of roses and sweet peas, branches of plum blossom and laburnum, and we made baskets of poppies and corn-flowers for the parish sale-of-work. Doctor Harris took lots of roses for his poor bedridden patients. I worked happily. There was a great sense of fulfilment in the occupation and even

Henry admitted he found it grew on him. It never palled on me. Many times in my life when I have found affairs getting me down, I have turned again to a few rolls of *crêpe* paper and a pair of scissors to find relief and comfort.

The day came at last when Doctor said he thought we might have a look under the splints. I was through the doldrums. The stinking puttee of plaster was cut away—and my, how that early plaster did reek! The splints were eased off and the leg exposed. Authority looked as if he was having kittens. Nobody spoke. Doctor Harris ran his hand down from knee to ankle, lingering where the break had been. The verdict came slowly. 'Lovely,' he said. 'Lovely. Green bones, green bones, they mend well.'

Liz and Cookie burst into tears. They were so happy. 'Champagne all round,' said Authority. Henry went with Cookie for the bottles and glasses. Doctor raised my shoulder that I might take a look at my pallid extremity with its scabby limpet of dried blood and lint. It was revolting and I was promptly sick. A fresh splint and soft dressing were applied and I was allowed to sit up in my bed for a while each day, and Mr Mulholland, the Curate, began my lessons again.

I enjoyed learning with him, he explained reasons so splen-didly, I knew why I was learning; somehow that seemed so very important. He was an Irishman, red-headed, freckle-faced —not dainty sunshine kisses, but hefty brown spots that didn't fade in winter. His eyes twinkled so much that you just laughed at nothing, and didn't know why.

Henry said he reckoned that the first Mulholland was a leprechaun, no less; it seemed likely. He was as tall as Henry. I used to think he was quite old. Maybe he wasn't; he was one of those people who seem always to be growing out of their clothes, raw-boned folk with sleeves too short and trousers that need lengthening. Cookie knitted him nice winter scarves which he invariable left at somebody's bedside. His landlady knitted his socks, the thickest grey worsted she could buy. They wouldn't stay up and they left a gap of hairy leg between sock and trousers. He went the rounds of the parish on a bike. It had no mudguards and had no working brakes. 'Sure, why brakes? I just stick my foot down.'

He was a wonderful curate. The sick swore he was better than a bottle of medicine and the dying went gently to their Maker under his guidance. He was a forthright apostle, a battling Christian; a handy man with a cricket bat on the green. Henry said he boxed like a gorilla. His football tackle was definitely Dublin University, and many a hop-picking bully knew the weight of his hand. Once, in a fit of curiosity most unbecoming, I asked him why he hadn't got a wife. He said 'Sure, mavoureen, there was once a colleen, but she liked the gay life, that's all.' He could sing, but not much tune to it. At beanfeasts and harvest homes or at parish concerts, his rendering of 'St Patrick was a Gentleman' always brought the house down.

He had schooled me for several years in arithmetic, English and geography, with some Greek and Latin. These two latter were not really considered suitable for female education; blue-stocking was almost a dirty word. Women were beginning to shed their shawls and footstools, Women's Lib was already a lusty infant causing men quite a lot of bother; for Pete's sake keep higher education away from womenfolk. Godfather used to laugh. He said, 'Bless 'em all. The more they learn, the better fun they'll be!'

After long weeks of idleness I wasn't too keen on lessons. Henry said I had been in the stable too long, got fat and lazy. If I didn't buckle to, I'd be put at the bottom of the class when I got to school and that wouldn't do at all. By the time October rolled round I was well up to standard in some subjects, way ahead in others.

CHAPTER TEN

The day before Authority and Liz took me off to school, Henry and I had a long chat in the potting-shed. I sat on the bench, whilst he stoked his clay.

The hour was cutting us both off from a phase that had become very precious. Nothing could take it away; the good wine was made, but baby days were gone. I felt it, and deep inside myself I was unsure, frightened to let go of a friend's hand. There were short silences between us whilst Henry drew inspiration from his old cutty. He said I was being seconded to a new Mess, must feel my way around for a while; that all Messes were different and their traditions had to be studied and respected. I must go slow and remember that the regimental sergeant-major's orders were absolute, whether I agreed with him or not. Above all, I must choose my off-duty company very carefully, and promise never to forget that I was being seconded from a crack regiment to which I owed myself and all I was.

With all he had said written on my heart, I promised faith-fully, before bolting for my private sanctuary under the laurels and in dark green secrecy and gloom having a darn good cry. I did belong to a crack regiment. I'd honour them to the end. They had shaped me, were all a part of me. From dear Authority I had learned to comprehend a power, greater than any other, to which I owed bounden duty. Henry had opened for me a window on all peoples under heaven, a family chain of humanity, endlessly making the same mistakes, endlessly mending them with the same poor tools, falling, to rise again, moving onwards, struggling upwards, pitiful at once in either failure or triumph. From my beloved Liz I had manners and deportment that could take me anywhere, a loving awareness of all creatures great and small, and of all that I must one day be as a woman. Yet, in spite of all that, I was naked as a new-born field-mouse in the world I was entering, epitomised by thirty select young ladies. It was a cattery.

The founders had, from the very start of the establishment, frowned upon the rising, wealthy, commercial families, but the present principals had been persuaded to accept the daughter of a fabulously wealthy European arms manufacturer. A florid, lumpy, girl she had a mass of yellow, frizzy hair, which she was permitted to wear loose, whilst the rest of us had to tie our pigtails well back. Everything she owned was just that little bit more exclusive than anything we had. Our white cambric nightdresses were just that, up to the neck and down to the wrists. Hers were Swiss, hand-embroidered with initials. I made a mental resolution to ask Liz to do my initials on mine before next term—but it never came to that.

By order of seniority she was head of the dormitory into which I was put. Six little white bedsteads in a row, facing six white washstands, with jugs and basins. Cold water in which to wash down with brown Windsor soap—as the weather got colder most of us made a scanty do of the 'up-and-down' and waited for the week-end bath night. A slop-pail and foot-bath, with a white chamberpot, stood below each washstand. In winter-time a maid entered at seven a.m., woke the girls and splashed a couple of pints of hot water into each bowl and left the slug-a-beds to let it get cold.

A strip of patterned carpet, dull greens and browns, ran the length of the room in front of the washstands, the rest of the floor was bare. No bedside-mats on which to linger; up and out. Beside each bed there was a chest-of-drawers, white like all the rest, supporting a small swing mirror and such treasures as we possessed. Hairbrushes and combs were kept in initialled linen bags. 'Money's' silver-backed hand-mirror was the envy of the dormitory. She would lend it sometimes to her current favourites. Rumour had it that she had arrived at the Academy with a dressing-case full of silver-topped bottles! Awful taste. It had been put into the strong-room; only the hand-mirror was left on her dressing-top. She was the lion. Her bed was at the far end of the room out of the draught. Mine was next to the door, an inhospitable spot. If I stayed on long enough, I would acquire the senior spot—small comfort when you couldn't keep the back of your head warm.

In the bed next to Money's was a permanent boarder, whose parents were in India. Authority knew them well. I knew her, she had been to parties at our place and had stayed once for a week's holiday. She was the current jackal to the lion. From my first entrance she was out to needle me. Remembering Henry's instructions, I played it low. I made polite overtures, without response. I felt I was indeed seconded to a darn funny Mess; I wrote and told Authority so. I felt homesick. It was almost the end of my first term, nearly three months on the strength, before I even began to find my voice, even do more than to whisper. Life was not profitable.

Then came the catastrophe. Money had a birthday. From Fuller's of Regent Street her parents ordered her a huge box of chocolates, hand-made, with heavenly centres. A black satin box! Magnificent box, tied with lush pink satin ribbons and with a garland of white velvet and satin roses with silver leaves. Proper totsy; what my Godfather called a stage-door box. We all admired its beauty as it lay on her bed. I don't think we envied her, she was after all to be lady bountiful.

Prayers were over, lights out, and we were all supposed to be asleep. The wall clock tinkled midnight. Money and the Jackal sat up in their beds; so did the rest of us. Money lit her candle, placing it on the floor to hide the light. The Jackal whipped out of bed like a long dog. Untying the ribbons, she crowned the birthday girl with the rose-wreath. Very fetching it looked too on the yellow hair; we applauded that. On Money's invitation we gathered round to sample the mouth-watering selection and to munch appreciation, when out of a clear sky came the thunderbolt.

One girl asked, 'May I take another, please? They're heavenly! Thank heaven for the man who invented chocolate. Who was it? Anybody know?' Off my guard in the excitement of the moment, I piped up casually, 'Oh, don't you know? It was the Aztecs, Mexicans, hundreds of years ago. There's a drug in it. If you eat too much of it you get hallucinations. Henry said so. He knows.'

The pearls of wisdom brought utter silence. Then Money drawled, 'And who on earth is Henry? Your schoolboy cousin? Your brother?'

The Jackal piped up spitefully, 'Good Lord, no! She hasn't got a brother. Henry's a drunken old gardener who works at their place. I've seen him.' I was stricken rigid by the insult to Henry. It was said with deliberate offence. There was a black, bitter taste in my throat that had nothing to do with chocolate. It was the taste of stone-cold fury, not a healthy, hot-blooded rage. Never again have I known such anger, thank God. I stared at the Jackal until she cringed, before I landed her a professional clout alongside her head that knocked her across Money's bed, capsizing most of the goodies to the floor. Inside seconds I was the centre of a catfight, silent ferocity, no holds barred. One lady had me by the pigtail, wringing like fury, another scored my cheek with her finger-nails. I took a clout on the nose and it made me fighting mad. I hit out; that really cheered me.

The candle went out. Skidding on chocolates we went down in a heap, to scrap savagely in the dark. Money stayed in her bed, hugging what was left of her birthday chocolates, *sauve qui peut*. I took a kick in the ribs and a jab in the eye from some-body's elbow. In utter agony I rolled under the Jackal's bed out of the fray. The others were still scrapping. I've often wondered why.

I got to my feet painfully between the beds to get my breath. Suddenly the dormitory door was flung open. Elderly Mamselle Janine stood there, a night-lamp in one hand, her Alexandra fringe in curling pins, night-cap askew, her enormous red dressing-gown draped to her waist. A real Cassandra. She stared, scandalised, at her young ladies! She started to scold us. 'Ladees! Ladees! Cet ees n'pas possible that you forget you are young ladees. What ees all thees? Answer me? *Non*? Ees eet that you cannot?' She stood waiting.

The Jackal found her tongue. Pointing at me she screeched, 'I didn't do a thing. She started it, Mamselle Janine. She hit me . . . she did! Didn't she?'

She appealed for support and got it! There was a chorus of, 'Oh, yes, Mamselle, she did.' That did it. There was no one on my side. Blood was trickling from my nose, pink chocolate cream oozing up between my toes. I suddenly felt dirty, defiled; I needed a bath. Money, anxious to do the right thing, hopped from her bed with the chocolate box and drifted to the door in her white nightie; with the wreath of white roses still on her hair she was like something off a church window. Sweetly she invited Mamselle to share her birthday treat.

Mamselle snapped, '*Merci bien,*' took one, grabbed me by the arm and marched me out. In the sanitary room I was cleaned up, patched up, and put to bed. Next morning I was told to stay where I was; I was evidently no fit company for the ladies. I got out of bed and had a peep at myself in the mirror. One black eye, completely closed, a nose the size of a Victoria plum, coloured like one, too. Three claw marks down one cheek, bruises all over me, and my right ribs so sore that I couldn't bear to touch them. Not a bad total, they'd done me over all right. Thinking over the scrap, I knew there must be quite a few bruises shared out by the others. Not bad, I thought. My first battle. Maybe I hadn't exactly won it, but it hadn't been sterile.

Late that same afternoon a maid-servant brought my outdoor clothes and shoes; I was to dress and go down to the front hall and wait. My luggage was being loaded on a hired cab. As I reached the hall, Authority was leaving the holy of holies. I heard him say, 'Good day, madam.' He took one look at my battered beauty, picked me up and carried me out to the cab. I never yet saw a man laugh so heartily. I was out on my ear. I was going home. But I didn't laugh. *Amour propre* must be respected. Authority was adamant that Henry must never know what had been said of him. I was taken to my Godfather's apartments in Piccadilly to spend a diplomatic three weeks in the care of his batman and wife.

It is wonderful what raw beef-steak, in the right hands, can do for a really classy shiner. Godfather talked the incident over with me and he thought I'd made a pretty good effort; the account of the punch-up he thought very funny. That bitter crack made by the Jackal didn't diminish Henry in my eyes; I only realised how mercifully blind I had been in my love, that I must remain blind, that the only way I could help him was by standing squarely beside him, supporting him. That was love and friendship. He was still my Henry, my alley marble.

Liz and Henry met me at Ashford on my return. They both

knew there'd been a shindig, that was all; that much Authority had seen fit to admit. I gathered hazily that I was seen as a bit of a black sheep, and maybe I was. Life slid once more into the old well-loved grooves; lessons with Mr Mulholland, gardening with Henry, plus a grand new interest three mornings a week with Cookie, learning the art of the still-room, cooking and housekeeping. There were two afternoons a week with Liz, knitting, doing crochet-work, fine embroidery, lace-mending and how to care for household linens. Joy above all this, Cookie allowed me the free run of her old household manuscripts and cook-books. Years later she bequeathed them to me, with love and her recipe for toilet water, the most delicate perfume I have ever found.

I mastered Middle English to be able to read those manuscripts, to learn that poached eggs and rissoles dated from the fifteenth century. So did game-pies, with the first rearing of a fine coffin of paste, and the recipe for this is just the same today; every little pork-pie in the shops, just the same. I also found that quince marmalade, shardequy, was 'much favoured as a help for pregnant women'. I couldn't persuade Cookie to tell me what it meant. I wasn't old enough to know.

CHAPTER ELEVEN

Whenever we made a summer trip to the coast we came back with a keg of oysters, either Faversham or Whitstable natives, for an oyster feast. My Godfather and Authority had a passion for oysters. They were reckoned as being *especially*—said with a nod and a knowing wink—'good for gentlemen.'

There was a famous oyster bar in Piccadilly, Scot's, where men-about-town gathered around midday for a dozen or so, washed down with stout, or chablis, and thus fortified, strolled along to a lunch date—part of the dilettante day of the stage-door Johnnies in an age long since past.

A keg of oysters, about three hundred according to size, cost us ten shillings, straight from the beds, fresh as a daisy, sir!

'OYSTER POWDER'

1700

Open your oysters. Remove the shells. Pound the fish in a mortar, adding salt in the proportion of one drachm to one dozen oysters.

After pounding well, rub through a hair sieve. Return to the mortar with as much flour, that has been completely oven-dried, as will make them into a paste, working the whole with your hands.

Flour your fish board, and roll your paste to the thickness of a crown piece. Divide into small square pieces. Lay them in a Dutch Oven, where they may dry without burning. Turn them every half hour, until they begin to really dry.

Crumble them and pound, in the mortar, to a powder, which sift and bottle carefully, well sealed, for use. Tightly corked, will keep for years.

Sprinkled on thin bread and butter, this makes delicious tea sandwiches.

A most delicious Sauce
for Boiled Chickens or Steaks

Put one ounce of Butter into a stewpan with three drachms of Oyster Powder and six tablespoons of milk. Set on a slow heat and keep stirring until it boils. Season to taste and serve, in a hot boat.

NEVER POUR A SAUCE ON A MEAT
BEFORE SERVING

By carrier's cart they were a few pence more. Favershams and Whitstables came in season in August and September, were at their best in October. With the keg between them and a bottle of chablis, lots of napkins and a bucket for empty shells, God-father and Authority would retire to the little summer-house by the lake to enjoy an oyster feast, opening the shells for each other turn and turn, until they'd had all they wanted. The remainder went to Cookie in the kitchen. She had cunning recipes for preserving them for use out of season; pickled oysters, smoked oysters, oyster catsup and strong essence of oysters, dried oysters for afternoon tea sandwiches and many other delicacies, beef-steak and kidney pudding with oysters and mushrooms. Sparrow pie with oysters was a regular autumn dish, greatly relished; those who had no oysters used sparrows and chopped belly pork, which was every bit as good.

Henry used to tell me that at the end of July all the sparrows took their nippers to the seaside, which was why, for about six weeks, we rarely saw them round the house. It's true; they did go on holiday, not to the seaside, but to the cornfields where ripening corn is free, where they gorged until they were fat and plump against the shortages of winter. With the corn carried and gleaning done, they returned to the stackyards. The genera-tion gap is no new thing: only the old 'uns came back. The youngsters, mostly the bachelors, formed new flocks.

Let there be no raising of shocked hands at the idea of eating the dear little sparrows. In some years they were a plague. Does not the Bible tell us that five sparrows cost one farthing all those centuries ago? Sparrows came into season just as did leverets, plovers, snipe, woodcock, young rooks, wood pigeon and partridges, mallard and teal and the occasional heron. All punctuated the countryman's gastronomic calendar. In some years farmers were ready to pay a penny a dozen for sparrows' heads. Many a laddie earned himself a few pence for Christmas 'spudger snatching' in the stackyards after dusk.

In making sparrow pie there was no nonsense like feathering

them. They were skinned and eviscerated in one operation. Only the breasts were used in pies, the ribs and trucks went into the ubiquitous stock-pot, the cook's companion on every range. No housewife in this tinned-soup age can have any idea what a stand-by a stock-pot was—everything went into it excepting vegetables and bread. It boiled all day and every day, was emptied and the contents strained off once a week. This solidified to a strong jelly; thick soup, clear soup, gravies and sauces, the foundation was at hand. It may not have been as quick as opening a can, but it was better nourishment and cheaper.

For more than a year my horizons had been steadily widening. I had entered my teens. Mr Mulholland told Authority that there was not much more he could teach me, that I had enjoyed far too individual an upbringing to profit from a school environment, I only needed two or three years of female polish, and that I was a 'broth of a Blister'. For himself he was going back to 'ould Oireland'. But Authority had left his heart in India and was considering another spell of duty there. So Godfather came up with the address of a lady in the north of England who took in half-a-dozen suitable young ladies—not ladees— for music and languages, protocol, painting and polish, and curtseys.

Liz took me to London and I was provided with a whole trousseau, and went out into the world, a wide, wide world. I loved it. I thoroughly enjoyed myself. It added spice and dimension to my holidays; cooking with Cookie, gardening with Henry and arguing relentlessly with everybody else. I even found spunk enough to contradict Mrs Vicar.

Henry didn't take kindly to the new pattern. I was told that he watched the carriage that took me to Ashford round the turn of the drive and beetled straight off on a binge that lasted a fortnight, and once more the Vicar's wife pestered him to sign the pledge. He must—or be damned! She deserved better than she got. He dodged her for some time but she was a determined woman and she asked the Vicar to speak to Henry. The Vicar was no torch-bearer. Henry was just Henry, not past praying for, but there are some things which really seem beyond the most fervent prayers. Authority just wished her luck when she complained that in his position Henry was such a shocking example to the other men. Poor old Henry. He wasn't a three-times-to-church-on-Sunday man, but he was a God-fearing soul, loving his neighbour as himself. All he wanted was to bear his cross in peace. She tried to interest Liz in her crusade. Poor darling Liz, who knew better than she did, that where devoted love had been powerless, what chance had a rabid T.T.?

One thing Liz did not know was that Henry was being pushed beyond the limits of polite endurance. There was some betting in the Bothy. Godfather laid a fiver with Authority that the Vicar's wife would win—constant dripping wears away a stone. Suddenly, to everyone's surprise, Henry's will broke. Yes, he'd sign—maybe. He played it low, grinned and said 'nuffin'. Godfather wrote that he was claiming his fiver, that he and Authority were getting out of the way for a bit. They went to Paris.

Cookie's letter said that Henry was to sign the pledge in the vestry on the coming Sunday evening before service. 'Fight the Good Fight' was the hymn; the churchwardens would be his witnesses. It didn't seem to me that Henry was going to have much to do with it, and I didn't see him going to the slaughter with a blue ribbon round his neck. What was going on?

Sunday night arrived and the church was full. This was an occasion, but neither Cookie or Liz went that night. Liz was low with an anxiety headache. Cookie had gone to see a friend in Faversham, well out of the way. The five-minute bell tolled for ten. No Henry. The service began, and finished—without Henry. He had retired to his only stronghold, the potting-shed. There, securely locked in, under the bench and tight as an owl, he was sleeping it off.

On their return from Paris, Godfather paid over his fiver,

and Authority was off to India. Once again Henry saw to his kit and horses, and once again took over the stewardship. A chapter was closed, the pattern altered. I didn't see so much of Henry, but he was always there. I was beginning to grow up.

I went on visits away, had my own guests to stay, with Liz as duenna. There were cultural trips, London, theatres, music halls and Paris with Godfather, operas, the Latin Quarter; new and exciting worlds, full of people and delight. Everything, everywhere, was full of change.

The Victorian era was one of enormous lop-sided expansion, which left the deep rural countryside to a large extent untouched. True, industrially acquired fortunes had caused the rise of a new type of gentry—as opposed to ancestral gentlefolk. These were people who had more pride than know-how. Wealth and power were the acolytes of a giant called progress. Better-ment for the masses lagged far behind. With the genesis of the great newspaper enterprises there came an up-and-coming con-ception of education for all. It spelt advancement, with the rise of the Trade Unions, with Labour representation in Parliament. The crowning achievement of the era was The Great British Empire, when we learned that everything coloured pink on the map of the world was ours! British! Never before had a country accomplished so much in a century.

That it had been a lop-sided accomplishment, producing a people slightly drunk on pride and power, didn't occur to those in power. In placid, rural areas, excepting where the overspill of town life impinged on his territory, or the great railway arteries offered day-trips to savour town life and ways, urban progress had not altered the countryman's way of life. Lanes were still pitch-dark at night, deep in mud all winter, choked with dust in summer. 'The palace of ease' was either a commode in an outhouse, or a chilly candle-lit trek down the garden after dark, and a bath was a shivering-pan on the bedroom floor, filled and emptied by hand. Paraffin at fourpence per gallon, Price's candles, twelves, tens, or eights, or farthing tallow dips, were the only household illumination. Working people went to bed early to save light—small wonder the birth-rate was high and large families the rule. In every household of any pretensions, each guest took a bedroom candlestick on retiring from the table at the foot of the stairs; and it was a whole morning's work for a houseman to trim, fill, and polish the chimney glasses of all the lamps used throughout the public rooms and hallways every night.

How often does one hear the remark passed today, 'What an awful way to live! How did people stand it for so long? All that dreadful hard work. Poor slaves. Just think how they lived! Imagine!' But my answer to that is, 'With what would they have filled their lives if there hadn't been work? Contentment may not make for riotous living, but it doesn't breed unrest such as we see today in this brave new world of unlimited gadgets.'

Nevertheless, the aristocratic image was blurring. In the rural communities change had been slow to start, the intense, almost passionate conservatism was being badly jolted. The feudal habit of thought was being attacked from all sides. The labourer blinked and raised his head where, for generations, he had bent his back. He was told that mastership was an accident of birth, not a divine dispensation. The foundations of his known world were being shaken; they are rocking to this day. A thin sighing wind was blowing through the corridors of time, a shifting wind; people were on the march.

I felt this but didn't fully apprehend why. There comes a time in every man's life when he feels he must stand and take stock of his prospects and past achievement, before time sits him in the chimney corner. Henry had reached this stage. We talked it all over in the old familiar jawing place. I, the new generation, saw his point of view, yet I didn't really think seriously that he would leave Authority, who was coming home for a spell. Godfather said he thought it was all part and parcel of the general unrest in the country; it would probably pass when Authority got back. It didn't pass, it simply went underground.

'THE CONFECTION'

A great spoonful on rising. Taking after one pint of Hot Broth, or such. It will not provoke Piles, though taken long.

Into a large Gallipot, with a close fitting lid, place one pint of Hot Water with one pound of Clear Honey. Stir to dissolve the honey. Grate eight nutmegs and add to the mixture, with one bottle of Madeira Wine. Stir well. Add thereto one pound each of Figs, Dates (stoned), Malaga Raisins, and fine Damask Prunes, with half a pound of Black Barbados Sugar. Three ounces of Senna, clipped small, and four ounces of best Spanish Liquorice.

Incorporate well, adding more Hot Water if you deem the fruit will take it.
Cover closely, with a paper under the lid. Set it in a warm oven, stew down until it becomes a thick Chutney, when add half a pint of Best Brandy.
Stir well, and whilst still hot, pot into convenient jars. Cover closely with Brandy Bladders. It keeps well.

CHAPTER TWELVE

With a more liberal-minded monarch on the throne, society was out of the Windsor apron-strings. The old image of close domesticity was vanishing. The weekend habit sponsored by King Edward the Seventh had caught on. All along the Kentish seaboard, beautiful bungalows were being built, within quick and easy weekend distance from London. Once a month the 'landsale' trains brought crowds of city speculators to purchase large plots of cliff-top chalklands. 'A fine plot, gentlemen, Number 65 on your plans. One hundred feet by thirty. What shall I say, sirs? Numbers 64, 65, and 66 twenty pounds each in one block? Thank you, sir!'

Commercially acquired money was being spent lavishly.

These new dwellings were not the brashy stuff that went up after 1918, but fine spacious homes set in lovely gardens, designed for entertaining. Henry turned longing eyes that way. He yearned to create those beautiful gardens. Affection and loyalty were the brakes on his ambitions but he still yearned on.

Prosperity was coming to areas where there had been little or no activity before. The fast expresses of the S.E. & C.R. spilled the worn-out businessmen on to the seaside platforms on Friday evenings at five o'clock and whisked them back to the metropolis on Monday morning. Stockbrokers, in morning coats and toppers, sported rosebuds from their gardens in their button-holes. Westgate, Margate, Broadstairs and Ramsgate boomed.

I still believe Henry would never have left us but for a most unfortunate incident, which probably caused long suppressed emotions to erupt violently. Owing to an attack of enteric fever during the Boer War, Authority was left with a persistent bowel trouble. Every morning he had to take a large tablespoonful of confection, which Cookie made by the half gallon in a huge gallipot which stewed away in the kitchen oven until the contents were a lovely, thick mush. Figs, dates, prunes, Malaga raisins, honey, Barbados sugar, nutmegs, senna and a bottle of Madeira, just stewed and stewed. A bottle of brandy, just before potting, finished the job. It was very effective. One large table-spoonful, taken fasting, chased down by a pint of hot coffee, and Authority sallied forth, with his mail and *The Times*—or the latest French yellowback—down the long ride to the west covert, where Henry and Billy Bennett had built for him a palace of ease. In one pocket he had a few Eley cartridges, under one arm his twelve-bore gun; and the red flag was hoisted.

At squatting height, a hole in the door was just at sighting level. There, safe from maids with slop-pails, he could sit and meditate, occasionally varying the monotony with a pot-shot down the ride. On darkish mornings, light under the trees was a bit tricky; the pastime had already cost him a couple of solatiums and two pairs of new corduroy britches.

On the day Henry gave notice it was the Drummer, Liz's old tomcat, who stopped the charge. He was an inveterate hunter; it had to happen some time. He'd had a long and lucky life. His youthful beauty had reached the gingery, rabbity grey of old age; amongst rough, tussocky grass he wasn't to be distinguished from bunny. It was poor Liz who found his body. She loved her cat and she raised Cain. With a lack of tact, absolutely out of character but prompted by his own distress at what he'd done, Authority offered to replace the Drummer with any kind of pedigree kitten she fancied. Poor man. He meant it well. It just wasn't the time to choose. Liz wept bitterly.

Her distress tipped the scales for Henry. He exploded like a charge of dynamite. It was six months' notice. He was leaving the place. It was an unalterable decision. A bombshell to all. Unbelievable! It couldn't be! Henry was a part of their lives. But it was true. He was going.

Six months later he and Liz were gone. Tom, 'the stick insect', his faithful shadow, chose to go with him and together they were to bring much beauty where so much of ugliness might have been. Henry went to his Mecca, the coastal gardens and landscape gardening.

I went with Cookie and old Mrs Dence to tell the bees that Henry was gone. It was the country custom to give the bees all news affecting the families they belonged to. The bee skeps were beautiful dome-shaped hives, made of plaited straw ropes, most delightful to see, each skep set upon its own little four-legged table, an air-hole in the roof of each one and an entrance-hole on a level with the alighting board.

For centuries man has reverenced bees as being very near to the heart of the Creator, little lower than the angels, living within their hives an orderly, judicial, communal existence, a civilisation that could put man's to shame.

Bees were free creatures not to be bought or sold. If a swarm of bees crossed to a neighbour's garden, you didn't fetch them back once they had settled. You might, seeing a passing swarm, try to get them to settle in a free spot—a roadside hedge—and you would do your utmost to prevent your own bees from swarming far afield. It was nothing to see a cottager following a swarm in early summer, banging a frying pan with an iron spoon, raising the very devil of a clamour simulating a thunder-storm. The queen bee is a delicate lady, she hates storms. Her servants gather round her and she must settle before it begins. A free swarm of bees was a responsibility, they became part of your family; you cherished them, gave them all the news. Almost every cottage garden had two or three skeps, some hung with bits of mourning *crêpe*, scraps of wedding-dress material, bits off Christmas trees. On the alighting boards could some-times be seen slices of wedding cakes or bits of funeral baked meats.

On the day Billy Maxted got married, his father put a dish-ful of sweet parsnip wine out for the bees. Next morning most of the bees were zizzling on their backs under the hive, wag-gling silly impotent legs in the sunshine. Mrs Dence called Maxted a wicked heathen. Who but a heathen would teach innocent insects to drink! She carefully set quite a few back on their legs, but they couldn't stand.

We had a dozen skeps on the east-facing side of the orchard, where the sun reached them early and they had a clear flight path. I felt that the bees would miss Henry because he was one of those people who can handle bees freely and never get stung. On early September mornings, when nights were chilling, I used to delight in watching him collecting handfuls of little wild bees off the wild scabious along the west covertside, where, gorged on nectar and reluctant to leave the last feast of summer, they had been overtaken by sunset and the quick chill of dusk. Scores of little silvery creatures with blunt, primrose bottoms, they crept all over his jacket sleeves whilst warming up for flight. It was wonderful to watch.

A very old gipsy woman, of the Kentish tribe of 'Love', once told me that only those near to God could handle bees. Women never! Gipsies could rob honey from any hives if they first rubbed hands and forearms with rosemary and lavender and then passed their hands over their face and neck. I still wonder whether she meant that gipsies were close to God, or that rosemary and lavender were the odours of sanctity. It's anyone's guess.

Authority was most deeply saddened by the departure of Henry. He had lost a comrade-in-arms, the friend of his heart. Godfather came down and spent several weeks with us. He said that Henry had gone to hunt peacocks while he could still run fast enough to catch one, and he wished him luck. We all did, but he had left a hole in our lives, a cut that was many months healing. It healed after a time and we were back on our even way. To my surprise I missed Liz terribly. I was growing up; I needed her. Jack Dence stepped into Henry's job, Cookie, as always, reigned supreme in the house. Jack was used to petticoat government, there were no more morning ructions in the kitchen.

The first decade of this century was almost spent, and peace was with us; we rejoiced that all was well. Was all too well? The blow fell. Edward the Peacemaker was dead. There were the funeral celebrations—and the Coronation of George the Fifth and Queen Mary; the tea-fights, the mugs and the fireworks. All in the garden was lovely.

For men of war, long periods of peace are frustrating and unsettling. Both Authority and my Godfather were feeling something of boredom, both wanted something they could get their teeth into. Authority was restless, hankering for the life he loved best. There was no country like India; not only that, neither he nor Godfather were getting any younger, neither would see fifty again. Godfather was sick of the sight of White-hall. He fancied a country life. He offered to take over the place as it stood; staff, stock and myself. He would bring me out. 'Give a dance or two, an' all that. Love it. No trouble at all.'

Both were evidently after peach pudden and peacocks. It was decided that when I was ready I should join Authority in Kashmir and run his household. But I couldn't see that being my fate. I wasn't cut out for a life of tea-cups and tea-cakes. I wanted wider horizons. After such an individual upbringing and education I wanted a constructive future. Man proposes, God disposes. I looked towards Fleet Street.

During the few years since they had left us I had made many visits to a happy Liz and Henry in their new surroundings; Henry heading for his sixties, prospering and highly successful, the artist uppermost at last, laying out beautiful gardens, lawns and flowerbeds, coaxing real beauty out of the hard Kentish chalk. Tom had married and lived nearby. The years were a smooth rise, creeping like thieves towards 1914 and the holo-caust. Sixteen years from war to war.

CHAPTER THIRTEEN

Few of us realised in that lovely summer of 1914 that our world was to be torn apart and that all we had known would never be the same again.

The Balkans were stewing up again; that was not new, they were a turbulent lot. Sarajevo was far away, the outrage a political nuisance. The Kaiser was an interfering old b——. Russia? Henry was profane. 'That bloody Kaiser, watch him. He's out for blood. He hated King Edward. He hates England. He doesn't give a damn about Serbia. It's us he's gunning for. Us. You mark my words. Treaty or no treaty.'

To the man in the street, treaties were made by men whose job it was to know what they were doing. Now, a treaty made in our names was landing us in the soup. From Continental spas, London society folk were scrambling back home. I had spent June and July with Liz and Henry on the Kent coast, and I had just got my feet into the street of ink. I interviewed some of them as they came ashore at Folkestone and Dover. Yes, it was serious.

The first of August, and Belgian refugees were landing all along the Kent coast from every sort of small craft, carrying everything they had been able to grab, from the week's laundry to the canary. Hastily convened committees of local ladies began to see that they were housed and fed. Liz got cracking. People began asking, were they all Belgians? Spy fever gripped even quite reasonable people.

I returned to London just in time to hear that England was at war with Germany. The rape of Belgium and the deliberate breach of treaty had killed all hope of peace. Henry had been right; the Kaiser was looking our way. London was shocked, reeling. It was a blow in the face. Recovery was swift. What followed must surely go down in the annals of our country as the most spontaneous, wonderful, amazing exhibition of love and loyalty ever seen, and may never be seen again.

Men, in a solid phalanx, packing the pavement in Whitehall. The rush to join up. The gentlemen of England. All gathering to repel a common enemy, Kaiser Bill and his son, Little Willie. All classes one in the face of England's need. Six and eight rows deep they stretched down Whitehall, along the Embankment, round into Northumberland Avenue, up the Avenue to the Strand, past the Lyon's Cornerhouse, back into Whitehall again; inching a slow, patient way, under the arch into the War Office yard to the shilling. The dotted line. All brothers. Bankers and city gents in spats and toppers, meat porters from Smithfield in straw hats and striped aprons, costers in pearlies and cloth caps, stockbrokers, and street-sweepers still carrying their brooms. Gentlemen and gentlemen's gentlemen, office boys from Fleet Street, haberdashers' assistants, little Jewish tailors from the East End, his lordship's butler and footmen, railway porters from Charing Cross Station, all to emerge as private so-and-so of so-and-such.

It went on for the best part of a week and all towns in England reported the same great response. They went, as iron filings, to the magnet of war, to a cruel adventure that bore no relation at all to their ideas of war. The cream and pride of the nation, a heart-breaking sight, said Godfather. Everybody was confidently predicting that it would all be over by Christmas, many were surprised when it wasn't. We were well into 1915 before we saw that it was to be a hard pull, that Kaiser Bill had prepared his assault well.

Godfather handed the place over as a military hospital. Cookie was a starched madam, in charge of the commissariat; she pushed the soldiers around a bit and enjoyed it. Godfather went to HQ in Paris; a brass hat, he said, pleased with himself.

Dig for victory. Henry's world went upside down. He was forced to destroy much that he had created. Velvet tennis courts became potato patches. Cherished flower borders produced onions and parsnips. He swore. He was still, at heart, a professional soldier. Growing spuds wasn't fighting. Once again time had passed him by. He was in his sixties. Too old! Too old! It was more than he could bear. In the bar of the New Inn he fought out battles with matchsticks on the counter.

A second Christmas was behind us, Easter looming and more and more men were gone from the village. Tom waited just long enough to see his first-born son laid in his mother's arms, before he too headed for Canterbury and joined the Buffs. Left with only one labourer nearly as old as himself, Henry grew bitter. There is no greater bitterness than that of willing old age shackled by the years. He was going more frequently to the pub. He watched volunteers go. 'Soldiers of the King, m' lads.' Saw them return on embarkation leave, enjoying brief glory, fraternal pints and backslapping. Saw some of them return again, in hospital blue. 'We've been, m'lads. We've seen, m'lads.' 'Patch 'em up and send 'em back!' Henry no longer fought matchstick campaigns in the pub. He sat, silent, listening to grim stories of mud and blood. It was no help to be told that they also serve who only dig and wait. It was festering destruction.

The Somme. Tom was gone. Blown to bits. Against such obscenity what was a boil and a hot pickle-jar? The news hit Henry hard. He had loved the foundling as a son. He grieved deeply, spending nights out on the clifftops, taking his bottles of beer with him, sitting drinking and brooding, staring out across the Channel towards the battlefields. With the wind in the right quarter the full boom of bursting shells came over the tide. He now went to the pub only to fetch his bottles. It's bad when a sociable man starts drinking alone. Something has to break. I felt I should go down and see what could be done. There was nothing. I returned to my job.

Life for me had become a long round of bedpans and soiled dressings, slop-pails and drawsheets. A V.A.D.'s life was pretty hectic. Coming off night-shift I found a letter from Liz. Henry was gone! Been missing for three days, without a word! Leaving no trace. She was sure he was dead, because he'd left his presentation watch and chain in the shed. He never went anywhere without them. Please help! Authority was far away, Godfather in Paris. I must go.

I scrounged a few days' leave and caught the next train from Victoria. There wasn't a clue. Where to start? He had vanished as surely as though he had never been. Questions, questions, questions. Was he dead? Was it suicide? Had frustration and liquor done their work? Was he wandering somewhere, bereft of memory, or had he fallen over the cliff in a tipsy stagger and been drowned? If he had, said local belief, he'd come sailing in on the tide in three weeks, when the drowned are supposed to rise to the surface and float. The coastline was watched, but he didn't arrive. He was gone. Prayers were offered for him in church. Brokenhearted, Liz went into mourning.

I could not accept that a man of Henry's calibre would take his own life. It didn't make sense. Failing his corpse, I went on hoping. There must be a reasonable solution. Back in hospital I talked it over with colleagues, who were of the same opinion. Godfather thought he might have wangled an unofficial crossing to France and be wandering round Etaples or somewhere; in which case he'd come to light sooner or later. We had done all we could.

After four long months of silence, an official packet was delivered to Liz, O.H.M.S., bringing papers from the War Office. The old warhorse was back in the Army! At the moment I got Liz's letter I could cheerfully have wrung his neck. Liz's opinion wasn't quotable. Months later he told me what had happened on the night he vanished. When Tom was killed, he had been consumed with a desire to avenge his death. The thought bedevilled him and drink couldn't drown it; he was being crushed under a burden he couldn't support any longer, so he sat on the cliffs night after night, as close to Tom as he could get, drinking himself blind, apologising to himself for being too old to go. Sitting there he argued that surely there must be someone who would understand how he felt and would listen to him.

Suddenly he knew the answer. Get back to Lichfield, his regimental cradle. Surely, they'd listen. He would tramp back to HQ and beg for the right to once more wear the Staffordshire rust. He saw nothing else but his central idea. He had enough money in his pockets to carry him along without booze, if he slept rough. If he got short he could do odd jobs on the way. There was nothing else in his mind. To think was to do. For the second time in his life he was jettisoning an existence he could no longer face. Solemnly he slung two dozen empty bottles over the cliffs into the sea and began the long tramp to the Midlands.

The journey took him eight weeks, clearing his eyes and hardening him up; much of it he couldn't recall. When he marched into HQ Lichfield he was a fit, smart man. Quality was manifest. He wanted a chance to serve again? They didn't ask his age. It was the heyday of the dug-out, of good stock, good education and exemplary record. They accepted him gladly. With sergeant-major's rank he began training men on Cannock Chase, and there began for Henry what I believe was the greatest period of self-fulfilment and satisfaction he had ever known; he was right off the booze for the duration.

I met the happy warrior in London on his first spell of leave, smart as paint in his khaki and leathers, his moustache waxed to the old imperial points, the well-remembered twinkle back in his eyes, his step jaunty as a lad's. I was proud to be seen with him. He demanded to see where I was working. I took him down to the hospital and introduced him to the girls who were off duty. They booked a box for the Bing Boys matinee. It was a riot. He joined in all the choruses. So did we. He fell hard for Violet Lorraine, and was, with great difficulty, persuaded against going round to the stage door—and nobody said, 'Oh! be your age.' He belonged to the great age of stage-door Johnnies. Dear Henry.

He gave us all tea at the old Strand Palace Hotel, where at his request the band played *Soldiers of the Queen*. With him an immense love of life and gaiety had invaded poor, dirty, sooty old London, like a gust of fresh air.

Later that night, as I waited to see him on his way down to the coast, he went mighty quiet. I asked what was wrong. He said he was scared of meeting Liz again. That made me laugh. He was meeting a new Liz and due for quite a shock, for Liz had gone to war, in the only way she knew, the mothering way. War brought to England fighting men from all the Colonies. To Kent came many thousands of Canadians to train before going to France and up the line. In batches of six, Liz billeted scores of them. She cooked, washed, mended and bullied those great husky backwoodsmen; and they worshipped Ma! She taught them how to care for sore feet and blistered heels. She doled out Beecham's pills and corn plasters, dosed them with cough mixture and saw that they were back in billets by ten thirty p.m. sharp, stone-cold sober, else they slept in the wood-shed. Sergeant-major or not, he'd have to toe the line with her boys.

After his leave was over, Henry admitted to me that his Liz was 'a fair corker'. That was something I'd known ever since the affair of the Pompey parasol.

Blood, mud, tears. The struggle went on. The Canadians had long been gone. The barrel was being scraped for men. The Yanks were in. Conscientious objectors were being sieved and screened, dodgers winkled out of safe jobs. For the first time in our history, women were being recognised as real, responsible citizens, called upon to do men's work; facing danger every day making munitions, plate-laying on the railways, lugging cargoes on docksides, humping luggage as porters, servicing locomotives, street-sweeping, emptying dustbins, matching up to the emergency with amazing adaptability. Adam began to realise that his rib was going to become a real challenge to his male supremacy. The ladies, God bless 'em, were proving equal to any challenge. Small wonder they couldn't be pushed back under the kitchen table.

When peace came again Henry returned to a business that was practically non-existent. All-out war had left nothing in hand for purely decorative, pleasure gardening. The destruction wrought by 'dig for victory' could never be set right. Money wasn't there, and neither was labour; he could not tackle the job alone. Hurt and bewildered he was too old to face the situation. He had eaten his peach pudden. In his emotional need a new 'Blister' entered his life. Once again he had a child to teach, to become his shadow as I had been, to be sat in the barrow with the tea-bottle and the tools. Little Tom adored him.

Henry still did a few odd job days, for very special clients. It was hard work. The countryside seemed to be dying. The rising generation wasn't going to start land work. Women could do that. Let 'em. Transport and garaging were the up and coming activities. War had established the petrol engine; it had finally proved itself. In the urgent struggle for peace the whole-sale change in our way of life had passed unnoticed. It would never be the same again. Old gods had been dethroned. Nothing was offered in exchange excepting scientific materialism. The older generations were bewildered, the younger ones heedless and over-enthusiastic, bent on having a good time to make up for what they thought they'd missed all the war years. The generation that should have been the leaven in the lump was lying in Flanders fields.

Henry served the gods he knew and trusted until the day he died. Gardening in his old uniform of khaki and puttees, his Sam Browne belt hung with his civilian 'ard 'at and gaiters behind his garden shed door, a little landscape planning came his way. He soldiered on, quietly. It was 1933.

Liz passed on in her sleep. It broke him. Tom's widow did what she could for him, but the clock was running down. Halt. Who goes there? Sorrow and old age caught him at his desk with the plan for a rose-garden on the board. We sent all his regalia down with him to rest. As I watched it sink below the level of the turf I thought surely Saint Peter would set him teaching little angels to fill thumb-pots. Dear Henry. Pass, friend. All's well.